It Is Written

"In the beginning was the Word, and the Word was with God, and the Word was God."

John 1:1 KJV

It Is Written

Poems & Testimonies Inspired By The Holy Bible

Patricia Middleton

IT IS WRITTEN

Cover Photo by istock.com/robynmac
Cover Design Leah Howse
Printed in the United States of America
2020

Published By
I Write The Vision dba
Poetricia Publishing
Collingswood, N.J.

ISBN 978 0 9801286 2 8
ISBN 0 9801286 2 5

Dedication

To

"Thy word is a lamp unto my feet, and a light unto my path."

Psalm 119:105

God

"Thy word have I hid in mine heart, that I might not sin against thee."

Psalm 119:11

Be

" Forever, O LORD, thy word is settled in heaven."

Psalm 119:89

The

"Grass withers and flowers fade: but the word of our God shall stand forever."

Isaiah 40:8

Glory!

"Heaven and earth shall pass away, but My word shall not pass away."

Matthew 24:35

ACKNOWLEDGEMENTS

In Honor of Phyllis Nicholson-Middleton

My Mother:
Mommy, you were my first example of what it means to be a Christian. You didn't just take us to church, but you lived what we learned, and you practiced what they preached. I live by that principle because of you.

In Appreciation of District Elder Mark E. Jones

My Father in the Gospel:
You instilled in me the importance of always *"rightly dividing the word of truth"* (2 Timothy 2:15). Because of your anointed teaching, I developed a true and sincere love for God's word. To this day, I remember, cherish, and practice everything I learned from you about the precious word of God. One such lesson is shared on page 164.

In Memory of Sister Ellen Pittman

My pre-teen Sunday school teacher:
She had a small stature, a quiet presence, and kind eyes. She was the first person who inspired my love for poetry. I guess she saw something in me, as good teachers often do, because she always gave me the longest poems to recite for the Annual Sunday School Easter and Christmas Programs. *That* was the beginning.

Special Recognition

Special thanks to Cassandra Ulrich:
I have always admired you as a poet and writer. Now I can add editor and proofreader to that list. Thank you for your support in the publication of this book.

PREFACE

The journey of publishing this book began over 20 years ago. I spent most of the 80's *"enjoying the pleasures of sin for a season"* (Hebrews 11:24-25). After a decade of wandering, I returned to my church home to continue my walk with Christ. It was a walk that began in my childhood but was detoured down another path of my own choosing. That detour ended in what I like to call a God ordained U-turn that allowed me to *"come to my senses and escape the snare of the devil" (2 Timothy 2:26)*. In September of 1990, I was refilled with the Holy Spirit, reclaimed into God's Kingdom, and ready to resume my walk with Christ. I was 27 years old.

Spiritually speaking, those were the most exciting years of my life. At the time my pastor, District Elder Mark E. Jones, had just begun a bible study on the book of Romans. Each week he taught *"precept upon precept and line upon line" (Isaiah 28:9-10)*. Because of his anointed teaching, I grew to love the word of God.

Shortly after my return, I realized that God had anointed my hands to write poetry. I had been writing poetry since I was 14, but not under God's direction. Up until then, I wrote under the leading of my own heart and mind. But once my heart and mind belonged to God, I began to write for Him. I was often called upon to recite poems at local church services, diocese meetings, and national conventions. People would ask me to write personalized poems for birthdays, anniversaries, weddings, and funerals. Sometimes the poetic tributes were recited, other times they were published in programs and commemorative journals.

As the years passed, I wondered *"What should I do with all these poems?"* First, I sold framed and laminated poems at our church's annual flea market (1994). Then, I published a poetry newsletter for single women called *The Companion* (1996-2002). Next, I created a line of poetry calendars, journals, and greeting cards (2002 to 2005). By 2008, I had written over four hundred poems. My first book, *A Time To Write,* was published in 2010. By May of 2020 I had published eight of my own books and 25 books for other independent authors.

But before all that, in the mid-90's, God gave me the vision for this book. Everything from the theme, to the layout, to a working title. And I've been working on it ever since.

After surviving a life-threatening illness in 2015, I realized that it was time for me to move forward with the publication of this book. I'm so grateful to God for blessing me to finish it. I hope I've made Him proud.

"Being confident of this very thing: that He who has begun a good work in you will complete it until the day of Jesus Christ."
Philippians 1:6 KJV

TABLE OF CONTENTS

Poems & Testimonies Inspired By The New Testament

INTRODUCTION

The title of this book comes from the account in Matthew 4:1-10 (and Luke 4:1-12) of the temptation of Jesus in the wilderness:

Matthew 4:1-10

Then Jesus was led up by the Spirit into the wilderness to be tempted by the devil. And when He had fasted forty days and forty nights, afterward He was hungry. Now when the tempter came to Him, he said "If You are the Son of God, command that these stones become bread." But He answered and said, ***"It is written****, 'Man shall not live by bread alone, but by every word that proceeds from the mouth of God.'" [Deuteronomy 8:3]*

Then the devil took Him up into the holy city, set Him on the pinnacle of the temple, and said to Him, "If You are the Son of God, throw Yourself down. For it is written: 'He shall give His angels charge over you,' and, 'In their hands they shall bear you up, Lest you dash your foot against a stone.'" Jesus said to him, ***"It is written****, 'You shall not tempt the LORD your God.'" [Deuteronomy 6:16]*

Again, the devil took Him up on an exceedingly high mountain, and showed Him all the kingdoms of the world and their glory. And he said to Him, "All these things I will give You if You will fall down and worship me." Then Jesus said to him, "Away with you Satan! ***It is written****, 'You shall worship the LORD your God, and Him only you shall serve.'"*
[Deuteronomy 6:13]

It's interesting to note that Jesus faced these temptations immediately following His water and Spirit baptism (Matthew 3:13-17), yet, once in the wilderness, He didn't rely on the strength of those experiences. With each temptation, Jesus relied on the word of God, specifically from the book of Deuteronomy—the same book that recaps the wilderness journey of the children of Israel.

In doing so, Jesus left us an example to follow—a principle for us to live by. When we find ourselves in a wilderness season, faced with the tests, trials, and temptations of the devil, we should always rely on God's word rather than our own spiritual strength. With each temptation, there will always be an answer in the word of God that will strengthen us and weaken our adversary.

My prayer is that the poems and testimonies in this book will not only uplift and inspire you, but also lead you directly to the word of God. For it is there that you will find the strength, the love, the peace, and the direction that you've been searching for. *It Is Written*.

POEMS & TESTIMONIES INSPIRED BY THE OLD TESTAMENT

"All Scripture is God-breathed and is useful for teaching, rebuking, correcting and training in righteousness, so that the servant of God may be thoroughly equipped for every good work."

2 Timothy 3:16-17 NIV

GENESIS

MY SISTER'S KEEPER

Genesis 4:9

"Where is your sister?" God asked of me,
Waiting for my reply,
And I didn't want to answer like Cain did
In times and years gone by.

Cain responded with sarcasm
Because he was guilty.
"Am I my brother's keeper?"
Maybe God expected him to be.

But jealousy of Abel's gift
Caused bitterness to take root,
And instead of dealing with his shortcomings
And the rejection of his fruit;

Cain blamed his innocent brother
And committed the first murder of all time.
He was the world's first hater, and centuries later
God was waiting for my reply:

"Where is your sister?" God asked again,
And He expected me to know,
Not just where she is, but how she is,
As life's seasons come and go.

Is she where I've already been?
Then I can help her along the way.
Is she trying to get where I am now?
Then I know just how to pray.

Since I have already overcome,
My sister's burdens, I can share.
I can lend godly assistance because
That's why God placed me here.

" Then the LORD said to Cain, 'Where is Abel your brother?'
He said, 'I do not know. Am I my brother's keeper?'"

Genesis 4:3-9

IN THE BEGINNING

Genesis 6:7-8 | Matthew 24:37 | 2 Peter 3:9

In the beginning God destroyed
The lives of women and men,
Who chose to live the life He gave them
Happily in sin.

The bible says corruption filled the earth,
And violence spread throughout the land.
Evil was in every thought,
And every imagination of man.

Wickedness was great upon the earth,
People ate and drank merrily.
They gave themselves in ungodly marriages,
They enjoyed sin continuously.

God began to regret that He created man,
It actually grieved Him in His heart.
He said *"I'll destroy man and the earth,*
But I'll save Noah with an ark."

Noah was a man who walked with God,
He was just and perfect in his ways.
He was the remnant of the righteous
And God looked on him with grace.

Today God is lookig upon this world,
With the same grace in His eyes.
While men and women everywhere,
Enjoy their sin-filled lives.

Corruption still fills the earth,
Violence is still rampant in the land.
Evil still fills every thought,
And every imagination of man.

Wickedness is still great upon the earth,
Sinners still eat and drink merrily.
People still give themselves in ungodly marriages,
And live life as though they were free.

And God has promised to destroy,
This evil earth once again.
He's not being slow about it,
He's just giving everyone time to make it in.

God is not slack concerning His promise,
He's giving all sinners a chance.
It's not His will that any should perish,
But that all should come unto repentance.

There is a way escape from destruction,
A modern day ark for all mankind,
It's in the death, burial, resurrection of
Our Lord and Savior Jesus Christ.

From the day of His ascension
To the day of His rapturous return,
We'd be ready when He comes or calls,
Or else be ready to burn.

For those still eating, drinking and marrying
Giving no thought about tomorrow,
Their end will be the beginning of
Tribulation and sorrow.

"So the Lord said, 'I will destroy man whom I have created from the face of the earth, both man and beast, creeping things and birds of the air, for I am sorry that I have made them.' But Noah found grace in the eyes of the Lord."

Genesis 6:7-8

"But as the days of Noah were, so also will the coming of the Son of Man be."

Matthew 24:37

"The Lord is not slack concerning His promise, as some count slackness, but is longsuffering toward us, not willing that any should perish but that all should come to repentance."

2 Peter 3:9

"I WILL SHOW YOU"

Genesis 12:1

Following the leading of the Lord, I began praying for direction regarding a new place of worship. God knew the desire of my heart was to belong to a church where I could continue growing to become *"perfected, established, strengthened and settled in the Lord."* (1 Peter 5:10)

Although initially I didn't know where to go, one day in prayer the Lord impressed a scripture upon my heart: *"Go unto a land I will show you."* (Genesis 12:1) I recognized the words right away. They were the same words God spoke to Abram so many years ago. I was comforted by the fact that God heard and answered my prayer. I knew that He would lead me to my next church home. I also knew it would not happen overnight. There would be some searching and some waiting. Searching for the right church and waiting for God to show me which one to join.

Confident that God would indeed show me, I began visiting a "short list" of churches that I comprised based on their location, statement of belief, number of years established, outreach in the community, and online presence. My time at each church lasted anywhere from one visit to three months.

After realizing the fourth church was not where God wanted me to be, sadness began to creep in. I cried out to God saying that I was tired of being without a church home and I was tired of visiting. In my despair, He answered so clearly and said, *"Go back to the first church."* When I did, during that morning service, He confirmed that it was indeed the church He wanted me to join.

Like Abram, I believed God and I left what was comfortable, convenient, and familiar, trusting that He would lead the way. And He did.

"And the Lord said to Abram, 'Get thee out of thy country, and from thy kindred, and from thy father's house unto a land that I will show thee'."

Genesis 12:1

"WHAT ARE YOU DOING WITH ISHMAEL?"
Genesis 17:18, 21

One Winter, several years ago, I was in the midst of dating an unsaved man. We had been seeing each other for about two years, and, although I didn't want to admit it, the whole thing was beginning to get to me. In the very beginning, during a period of fasting and prayer, God's instruction was loud and clear: *"Be his friend."* That was the first warning. But a month later when he invited me out to dinner for Valentine's Day, I agreed.

As time went on, he began to mention marriage. I refused to discuss the matter seriously because he still wasn't saved. Instead, I began creating scenarios which I thought would be conducive to him receiving the gift of the Holy Ghost. Our dates became a series of revivals, concerts, and banquets where I knew God's word would be preached and an altar call would be made. It didn't take long for me to realize that doing this was getting me nowhere.

Then I received the second warning from God. We were in the car and in the middle of yet another disagreement about him coming to morning service with me on a regular basis, instead of every once in a while. All of a sudden, a particular Donald Lawrence song came on the radio and I knew right away God was speaking to me. The lyrics were, *"I am God, All by myself, I don't need any help."* I immediately felt conviction, but once again I brushed it off, and continued my quest of *Saving Ishmael.*

During this time, my daughter was away at school and my son worked second shift. Most nights I'd come home from work, plant myself in my favorite living room chair, and have my evening prayer and devotion. On one such evening, in the midst of my meditation, the Lord clearly and distinctly asked me: *"What are you going to do with Ishmael when Isaac comes?"* Before I could ponder or even respond He added, *"Isaac is coming."*

Needless to say, waves of shame, guilt and regret flooded me like never before. For years I had testified that I was waiting on the Lord, that I wanted a saved husband, but my actions were speaking louder than my words. My actions were saying that I stopped believing Isaac was coming and was ready to settle for Ishmael.

Like Abraham, I received a prophetic word from God years before that *"a husband is coming"* but somewhere along the way, I stopped believing. This is why, like Abraham, I was desperately clinging to Ishmael, hoping to make him the promise. But once I heard the Lord's rebuke, I could not ignore it.

I began to repent and to seek forgiveness for not being obedient when God told me to *"Be his friend."* After that I began praying that he would break up with me. I couldn't bring myself to end the only dating relationship I'd had since I was reclaimed. Three times the Lord warned me, yet I stayed in the relationship for quite some time. Months later – many months later - I scraped together enough courage walk away from the relationship.

The following year, "Ishmael" called me to tell me he had joined a church, gave his life to Christ, and was getting married. That was a hard pill to swallow, but I realized that "Ishmael" was never mine to begin with. I learned the hard way that what God has for me is for me, and what is not for me is not for me, no matter how hard I try to make it otherwise.

I'm grateful to God for every time He speaks to me—whether it's a word of comfort, direction, instruction, or chastisement. In either case, it only reiterates His love, because *"the Lord disciplines the one He loves, and chastens everyone He will receive."* (Hebrews 12:6)

"And Abraham said 'Oh that Ishmael might live before thee'."
"And God said 'I will establish my covenant with Isaac'."
Genesis 17:18, 21

THE APPOINTED TIME

Genesis 21:1-2

Remember the life of Abraham?
He is called the Father of faith.
When God told him to pack up and move out,
He did not hesitate.

God said, *"Leave your family behind,*
With the exception of your wife."
Abraham consented to the voice of the Lord,
And set out to start a new life.

Of the destination, God only said,
It is a land *"I will show unto thee."*
Abraham didn't ask where the land was,
He just allowed the Lord to lead.

When God declared, *"From your seed,*
I will a make of thee a great nation."
Abraham didn't ask how, he just built an altar
And praised the God of his salvation.

But after twelve years passed without a change
To Abraham's family line,
He gave in to his wife's insistance
To follow the customs of the time.

His wife's maid, Hagar, became a surrogate
And through her, a baby boy was born.
Abraham and Sarah were both filled
With happiness and joy.

Then thirteen years later God spoke again,
"Sarah shall bear thee a son,
And in him shall all nations be blessed,
He will be the chosen one."

Abraham said *"What about the son I have now?*
I just don't understand."
But when God says He's going bless,
He doesn't need the help of a man.

Though Sarah was 90 years old and barren
God said, *"Is anything too hard for me?*
I will return at the appointed time,
And Sarah will conceive."

The Bible says that at the appointed time,
Sarah, in fact, did conceive.
It was almost 25 years from the time
That Abraham first believed.

Like Abraham, we've all asked the Lord.
In prayer for a certain thing,
And God speaks right back to us,
With the promise of a blessing.

Much to our disappointment,
Months and years begin to roll,
And what we *knew* what the voice of God,
Becomes what we *thought* we heard from the Lord.

Some of us also try to help God out,
By taking matters into our own hands.
Creating our own Ishmael blessing,
Hoping that God will understand.

But it's during these times we should realize
That God moves at His appointed time
We can't do anything to speed the blessing up
And no one else can push it behind.

But there is an Isaac blessing from above,
And no matter how long it takes,
We can be confident in God
That it will be worth the wait.

"The Lord visited Sarah as He had said, and the Lord did for Sarah as He had spoken.
For Sarah conceived and bore Abraham a son in his old age,
at the set time of which God had spoken to him."

Genesis 21:1-2

JUST LIKE JOSEPH

Genesis 39:2-3,21,23

Like Joseph, God gave me a vision,
Of what was to become of me,
I didn't realize that before it happened,
I'd be in my own prison of misery.

Like Joseph, I told everyone who would listen,
Of the great things that God had in store,
But when trials and trouble followed,
I had no idea what it was all for.

Like Joseph I wondered why God allowed,
So much trouble to enter my life.
Pain, sorrow, disappointment,
Heartache, worry, and strife.

I didn't understand how God could watch me
Struggle to discover His will.
No matter how much I prayed and read His word,
I still felt unfulfilled.

After I had done all I knew to do,
I'd fall on my knees in prayer,
Crying out to God in confusion,
Crying out to God in despair.

And each time I went down crying,
Not once did I fail to find,
Jesus waiting there to uplift me,
And to ease my troubled mind.

He brought His word to my remembrance,
I felt His presence each time I cried.
I felt His spirit, like arms, holding me.
I heard His voice say, "I'm right by your side."

Through every day of my suffering
Of my pain and misery
Just like He was with Joseph
The Lord was also with me.

"The LORD was with Joseph, and he was a successful man;
and he was in the house of his master the Egyptian.

And his master saw that the LORD was with him
and that the LORD made all he did to prosper in his hand.

But the LORD was with Joseph and showed him mercy,
and He gave him favor in the sight of the keeper of the prison.

The keeper of the prison did not look into anything that was under Joseph's authority,
because the LORD was with him; and whatever he did, the LORD made it prosper."

Genesis 39:2-3,21,23

FOR MY GOOD

Genesis 50:20

As I look back over this year,
I look back on many things.
Days and nights and hours,
And the moments they did bring.

I see days that went very well,
When things went according to plan.
I see nights that were quiet and peaceful,
When happiness was at hand.

Then I look a little closer,
And other moments appear.
Moments when I couldn't see at all,
Because my eyes were filled with tears.

Days that felt like doomsday,
Nights that never seemed to end.
Depression and fear running rampant,
And then, I look again.

And I see the hand of God,
Working things out for my good.
Allowing certain things to happen,
So I'd know that only He could:

Only He could give me the strength to smile,
When my world was caving in.
Only He could make me want to do right,
When I was tempted to fall back to sin.

Only He could give me the courage to stand,
When my world was falling apart.
Only He could whisper passages of His word,
Lovingly into my heart.

Only God could take a painful day,
And turn it into a day of praise.
Only He could safely lead,
When I couldn't see the way.

In all of this I can see
That God was working things out for my good.
Pulling out of me what shouldn't have been there,
And putting in me the things that should.

Pulling out fears of the future,
Putting in faith in Jesus Christ.
Pulling out worry and anxiousness,
Putting in patience and peace of mind.

Yes, as I look back over this year,
I realize now that all along,
God was making something right,
Out of everything in me that was wrong.

For all of my tests, trials and temptations
All that I preach, teach, and testify,
Were not only meant for my good,
But to save much people alive.

"But as for you, you meant evil against me; but God meant it for good, in order to bring it about as it is this day, to save many people alive."

Genesis 50:20

NUMBERS

WE ARE WELL ABLE

Numbers 13:27-29;30-33

Long ago from a burning bush,
God spoke these prophetic words:
"I have seen the affliction of my people
And their cry I have surely heard.

"So I will come down and deliver them,
Out of the Egyptians hands.
I will lead them up, out, and into,
A good and very large land.

"And not just any old piece of land,
But this land will surely be,
A place called Canaan,
That flows with milk and honey."

After God spoke these words to Moses,
He did, in fact, lead Israel out.
By night He guided them with a pillar of fire,
And by day, a pillar of cloud.

When at last, Canaan was before them,
Moses sent twelve spies out to view,
The land from a mountain top,
And they with conflicting news.

Ten spies said, *"It flows with milk and honey,*
It took two of us to carry this fruit!
But the people are stronger than we are,
And their cities are well fortified, too!"

Two spies - Caleb and Joshua -
With complete faith in God's plan,
Said, *"Let us go up at once, for we are well able,*
To possess and overcome the land!"

That was the moment to give thanks to God,
For His promise was coming true.
But just like Eve was tricked by Satan,
Israel fell for an evil lie too.

The ten spies spoke back with fear,
"There are giants living in the land!
They said, *"We all look like grasshoppers,*
Compared to the average man!"

The Israelites fell for an evil report,
And their blessing was further delayed.
We must let their story be a lesson,
And never let doubt get in our way.

We must not allow Satan to trick us
Into believing God's promises aren't true.
For when God's word goes out of His mouth,
It accomplishes what it was sent out to do.

So look for your milk and honey blessing,
And when it finally comes your way,
Remember, you too are well able,
To go up at once and possess it today!

"Then they told him, and said: 'We went to the land where you sent us.
It truly flows with milk and honey, here is its fruit.

Nevertheless the people who dwell in the land are strong;
the cities are fortified and very large; and we saw the descendants of Anak there.'

Then Caleb quieted the people before Moses, and said,
'Let us go up at once and take possession, for we are well able to overcome it.'

But the men who had gone up with him said, 'We are not able to go up against the people, for they are stronger than we.' And they gave the children of Israel a bad report of the land which they had spied out, saying, 'The land through which we have gone as spies is a land that devours its inhabitants, and all the people whom we saw in it are men of great stature. There we saw the giants (the descendants of Anak came from the giants); and we were like grasshoppers in our own sight, and so we were in their sight'."

Numbers 13:26-28;30-33

DEUTERONOMY

THROUGH THE WILDERNESS

Deuteronomy 1:2; 8:2-3

Like Israel, I was a slave,
My master's name was Sin.
And not until Jesus brought me out,
Did I have peace within.

I too was afflicted with burdens,
There were demons tormenting my soul.
Until the man with the keys to death and the grave,
Said, *"Let my daughter go."*

Just like God had promised Canaan to Israel,
I knew that God will lead me to
My very own place in His kingdom,
Filled with milk and honey blessings too.

But God took me through the wilderness,
And with each and every test,
I'd cry out unto the Lord,
"How am I gonna get out of this mess?"

The Lord chose not to answer me,
He wanted me to trust in Him.
He had already proven Himself to me,
When He delivered me from sin.

But in my wilderness, it was hard to trust God.
All I did was murmur and complain.
And just like that prolonged Israel's journey,
For me, it did the same.

In my wilderness, all my wells ran dry.
There was no water to be found.
I was thirsty for a fresh anointing,
But it didn't feel like God was around.

In my wilderness, I suffered malnutrition,
Mountains high and valleys low.
High in worry, low in spirit,
It felt like I had no place to go.

But God was merciful and gracious,
One day He heard my cry,
And came down and reminded me,
That He had been there all the time.

God fed me with the manna of His word,
Even though I had murmured and complained,
And to fill up my spirituall dry wells,
He showered me with His anointing again.

Now, after years in the wilderness,
In some ways I'm still going through,
But now I am confident than in due season,
I'll receive a milk and honey miracle, too!

"It is eleven days' journey from Horeb by way of Mount Seir to Kadesh Barnea. And you shall remember that the LORD your God led you all the way these forty years in the wilderness, to humble you and test you, to know what was in your heart, whether you would keep His commandments or not. So He humbled you, allowed you to hunger, and fed you with manna which you did not know nor did your fathers know, that He might make you know that man shall not live by bread alone; but man lives by every word that proceeds from the mouth of the LORD."

Deuteronomy 1:2; 8:2-3

JOSHUA

"BE OF GOOD COURAGE"

Joshua 1:5-6a

One Spring, many years ago, the public transit system was on strike, and I was forced to walk to work for almost a month. As I walked through the beautiful neighhoods towards center city, I began noticing "For Sale" signs. Soon, the strike was over and life went back to normal. But in that short time, a desire had been birthed in me. So, I met with a realator and began looking at houses in the hopes of becoming a first time home buyer.

After a few weeks of looking at houses, I had a dream. In it, I was in a church service and an usher tapped me on the shoulder and whispered that I was wanted on phone. I walked out of the sanctuary and grabbed the hanging receiver of the pay phone in the vestibule. The person on the other end said he was calling to confirm that the speaker, Minister Osmond, was on his way. I was confused because the person I was talking was supposed to be the speaker. He repeated that Minister Osmond was on his way and hung up.

A few days later I got a call from my realator asking me if I wanted to look at more houses, or if I wanted to make an offer on one of houses we already looked at. I was about to say "I want to look at a couple more houses" when she cut me off and said, "What about the house on Osmond Street?" I gasped, realizing immediately that the dream was a divine sign to let me know which house to make an offer on. I said, "That's my house! That's my house!" And told her I was ready to make an offer.

She tried her best to dissuade me from saying it was "my house." She told me that I shouldn't get my hopes up high, because I might be disappointed. She said she had seen things go wrong with other clients and ended her warning with an ominous "You never know." But she didn't know my God. She didn't know that God had given me a dream that confirmed my house was on Osmond Street. So I was sure beyond a shadow of any doubt that it was indeed "my house."

But gathering together financial records, being scrutinized by the realtor, the mortgage company, the home inspector (and everyone in between) was more than I could handle. Then once the closing date was scheduled, the mortgage company questioned a delinquent bill on my credit report from a few years before. I explained what happened, to the best of my recollection. Being a single parent of twins with no income but my own, I did my best, but sometimes I fell behind. They did not want to hear it. I was emailed a fabricated story "explaining" the delinquent item, a fax number, and told, "Print it out, sign and date it, and send it over right away, or we can't promise what might happen."

I can still see myself walking into the bathroom at work to pray. (You know we all have that favorite "prayer stall," right? Smile). I said, "Lord, I know that I don't have to lie in order to receive any blessing You have for me. Please help me in Jesus' name!" The voice of the Lord spoke back to me clearly, saying, "Be strong and of good courage."

Right away I recognized those words. They were the same words God spoke to Joshua after Moses died. God chose Joshua to lead the children of Israel the rest of the way to the promised land.

I wiped my tears, straightened my shoulders, walked back to my desk, and grabbed a piece of paper from a nearby printer. In my own handwriting, I wrote down the same explanation that I had previously told them, the truth that they said was "unacceptable." After signing and dating it, I took a deep breath, walked over to the fax machine, pushed "Send" and went about my business.

A few weeks later, on a snowy day in February my children and I moved into our new home. On Osmond Street. The realtor's last words to me were, "I have never met a client with that much faith."

"...No man shall be able to stand before you all the days of your life; as I was with Moses, so I will be with you. I will not leave you nor forsake you. Only be thou strong and of a good courage..."

Joshua 1:5-6a

BY GOD'S WORD

Joshua 1:8

Sometimes I go through life's storms,
Disappointments and distress,
And God gives me a scripture
To believe in and to trust.

Other times, like a drowning man,
Flapping his arms around in the storm,
I desperately reach out for
A passage on which to hold.

A verse or two to keep me afloat,
Until I can make my way back to shore,
And each time I do, by God's word,
My soul is safe from harm.

"This Book of the Law shall not depart from your mouth, but you shall meditate in it day and night, that you may observe to do according to all that is written in it. For then you will make your way prosperous, and then you will have good success."

Joshua 1:8

RUTH

THE TRUTH ABOUT RUTH

Ruth Chapters 1 through 4

(A rap written during my tenure as youth president 1994-2000)

Once upon a time in the Bible days,
A woman named Ruth paved the way,
For the birth of David—a man after God's heart,
But let me run it down to you from the start:

There was a famine in the land of Bethlehem,
That this one family just could not stand,
Her husband Elimelech moved them to Moab.
That was the last move he ever had.

Soon after that, Elimelech died.
Later his sons chose Moab women to be their wives,
And along with Naomi, their widowed mother,
For ten more years they all lived together.

But not happily ever after, because then the sons died,
While Orpah and Ruth, their Moab wives,
Were left with Naomi, their mother-in-law,
To return to the land of Judah.

Now before they left, Naomi said,
"Go back to your families, your husbands are dead."
She kissed them both goodbye, and they all wept,
But when Naomi looked up, they still hadn't left.

She added, *"Look, I'm too old to have any more sons,*
Or even another husband, my days are done.
And if I had more sons, would you wait 'til they were grown?
I think not, girls, so you'd best be gone."

Again they cried tears that they couldn't control,
This time when Naomi looked up, Orpah had rolled.
So she said to Ruth, *"You go on ahead."*
But Ruth replied, *"I'd rather stay with you instead.*

"Please don't make me leave you,
Don't make me stop traveling with you.

Where you go, I'll go; where you lodge, I'll lodge;
Your people will be my people and your God will be my God;

Where you die, I will die, and there I will be buried.
Nothing but death will separate you and me."

So, back to Bethlehem they both went,
Where the city was beginning the Barley Harvest.
Naomi changed her name to Mara because
She said she had been afflicted by the Lord.

Some time later a relative of Elimelech,
Let Ruth work in his field and he agreed to protect,
Her from the others in the field picking corn,
A job that daily left you weary and worn.

But you see, Boaz, was a distant relative,
He told Ruth, *"In all the years I have lived,*
"I've never met anyone with a love like yours.
The Lord God of Israel has for you a great reward.

Though you're a stranger, I've heard all about you,
How you stuck with Naomi, though you didn't have to,
You left your native land, and your family,
Just to settle in this unknown country.

For all you've done, God has instructed me,
To make sure that all is well with thee.
That's why I allowed you to pick from my field,
And why no one bothered you while you were here."

I'm sure that Ruth was overwhelmed by this,
Touched by something that she couldn't dismiss.
She told Naomi of all that had transpired,
And got approval to keep working in his fields for a while.

But as time went on it became very clear,
That Ruth was someone Boaz held very dear.
She made her feelings known, and Boaz asked for her hand,
But she was a part of Naomi's inherited land.

And apparently there was another relative
Closer in line, and who still lived,
That Boaz had the first chance
To accept or reject Ruth and the land.

So Boaz found the relative and ten witnesses,
And said, *"Sit down man, here's what the deal is:*
"Naomi's back to sell a parcel of land,
If you don't want to redeem it, I'll take it off your hands."

After a few words the relative closer in line,
Said, *"Boaz, that will be just fine,*
"I've got my own inheritance to look forward to,
You can redeem the land, and you can marry Ruth!"

Then to confirm that the deal was done,
According to the ways of their custom,
He reached down to his shoes and plucked off one,
This was all witnessed by everyone.

So Boaz took Ruth to be his wife,
And all of the people were satisfied.
God blessed their union with a new baby,
Named Obed, and he turned out to be:
The father of Jesse, whose shepherd son,
Became King David, the one and only one.
And fourteen generations later, through his bloodline,
Came the birth of the Savior of all mankind.

So, in the end, we find from this family tree,
A moral, a meaning to this true story.
Ruth was loyal to Naomi, so she received a blessing.
God used her in His plan to raise a King.

I end this with a message for me and you,
Something in life that you'll always find true:
It pays to show kindness and love these days,
Because God may use you in a special way.

*"So Boaz took Ruth and she became his wife; and when he went in to her,
the LORD gave her conception, and she bore a son.
And they called his name Obed. He is the father of Jesse, the father of David."*

Ruth 4:13,17

PSALM

IN THE WEE HOURS

Psalm 5:3

In the wee hours of the morning,
I heard the Lord calling me.
So I woke up from my sleep,
And fell down on my knees.

As I began to worship,
The tears began to fall.
I praised my King of Kings.
I praised my Lord of lords.

I thanked Him for His mercy,
That woke me up that day.
I thanked Him for His grace,
That kept me from harm's way.

I thanked Him for His love,
Faithful, true and real.
I thanked Him for meeting me,
In the wee hours as I kneeled.

"In the morning, O LORD, you hear my voice;
in the morning I lay my requests before you and wait in expectation."

Psalm 5:3

HEAVEN'S VIEW
Psalm 19:1

Although scriptures plainly state,
"The heavens above declare
The glory of God's handiwork."
I still was not prepared.

It was my first trip in an airplane,
I'd been afraid to fly for many years.
But what I saw from the sky,
Filled my eyes with tears.

Not tears of fear, I was no longer afraid,
The fear had been released.
All I felt from my window seat,
Was a surprising sense of peace.

Not nervous tears - the butterflies were gone -
These were tears of praise.
All I could whisper was *"God is great,*
And greatly to be praised!"

How could I feel fear as I beheld
Clouds God created long ago?
How could I be worried about turbulence,
When it was just God's wind a blow?

The nonchalant faces of passengers,
Amazed me to no end.
Laptops, novels, crossword puzzles,
Oh, how small the minds of men.

Didn't they realize they were flying,
Over clouds that my God made?
The same clouds that Jesus Christ
Will break through some day?

Up here I'm closer to the stars God made,
And the sun, and moon, and sky.
How could I ever have been afraid
Into His atmosphere to fly?

Looking out of my little window,
I had but one thing more to say,
"I feel a little closer to Jesus
Than I did on yesterday."

From now on whenever I fly,
This is what I'll do:
I will always reserve a window seat,
For a glimpse of heaven's view.

"The heavens declare the glory of God; And the firmament shows His handiwork."
Psalm 19:1

LET THE WORDS OF MY MOUTH

Psalm 19:14

Let the words of my mouth,
The rhythm and rhyme,
Be in sync with Your spirit,
Praising You all the time.

Let the words of my mouth,
The style and the beat,
Never cease to tell others,
About Calvary.

Let the words of my mouth,
My inflections and tone,
Testify that I am saved,
By Your grace alone.

Let the words of my mouth,
Be acceptable in Thy sight,
You're my strength, my Redeemer,
And the Lord of my life.

"Let the words of my mouth and the meditation of my heart
be acceptable in Your sight, O Lord, my strength and my Redeemer."

Psalm 19:14

[Dedicated to TAPS (The Apostolic Poets Society), a faith based poetry group]
that encourages, supports, edifies, and showcases the Christian Poet.]

THE GOOD SHEPHERD

Psalm 23:1-6

The Lord is my Shepherd,
I don't want for anything.
He will supply all of my needs,
He is the King of Kings.

The Lord is my Shepherd,
And like sheep in pastures green
Beside still, calm waters
In Him I have peace.

The Lord is my Shepherd,
He daily restores my soul,
And leads me in the righteous path,
Where I'm safe, strengthened, and whole.

The Lord is my Shepherd,
Therefore, no evil will I fear.
Through the valley of loss, grief, and death
My loving Savior is always there.

The Lord is my Shepherd,
With His rod and staff, He guides me.
Showering me with blessings
Despite the plans of my soul's enemy.

The Lord is my Shepherd
He covers me with the oil of His anointing.
For my heart, mind, and soul's protection,
And for my spirit's healing.

The Lord is my Shepherd,
In His house I shall always abide.
His goodness and His mercy will follow me,
All of the days of my life.

"The Lord is my shepherd; I shall not want.
He makes me to lie down in green pastures; He leads me beside the still waters.
He restores my soul; He leads me in the paths of righteousness for His name's sake.
Yea, though I walk through the valley of the shadow of death,
I will fear no evil; for You are with me; Your rod and Your staff, they comfort me.
You prepare a table before me in the presence of my enemies;
You anoint my head with oil; my cup runs over.
Surely goodness and mercy shall follow me all the days of my life;
And I will dwell in the house of the Lord forever."

Psalm 23:1-6

"SAY THE 23RD PSALM"
Psalm 23:1

The voice was unmistakable. *"Say the 23rd Psalm."* I heard it over the music blasting from my radio. I heard it over the "buzz" I had from the three Long Island Ice Tea drinks I had an hour earlier at the club. I heard it over the fussing and cussing going on in my head because he stood me up.

Yes, I heard the voice over all of that while driving under the influence on Lincoln Drive in Philadelphia, PA. It was a long curvy road next to water that spilled into another long road with more of the same: curves and water (East River Drive, now Kelly Drive).

When the voice said, "SAY THE 23rd PSALM" I snapped out of my haze, immediately rolled down my window, switched the radio from the music station that was on to a local news station (don't ask me why), and repeated the 23rd Psalm over and over all the way home.

Though I was far from God, I knew that if I didn't obey that voice, I would die that night. But even in my sin, God was covering me. Four years later, I rededicated my life to the Lord, and as Apostle Paul once said, "Having obtained help of God, I continue to this day." (Acts 26:22)

"Yea, though I walk through the valley of the shadow of death,
I will fear no evil; for You are with me;
Surely goodness and mercy shall follow me all the days of my life."

Psalm 23:4,6

THERE WILL BE PRAISE

Psalm 34:1

Throughout the scriptures and throughout my life
This much I've found is true,
No matter what season I find myself in,
I must give God the praise He's due.

When I was discarded like Leah,
Because another was preferred over me,
Through pain and disappointment ,
A Judah praise was birthed out of me.

When my heart feels as barren as Hannah's womb
And I don't have words left to pray,
In bitterness of soul, as I weep to the Lord,
Even then, I find there is praise.

Like Job when there's a loss so unfathomable
So great and so out of the blue,
And I feel on the verge of losing my mind,
There is still praise left for You.

Like David, when I go against God's will,
And the wages of sin should be my reward,
After correction, and a reaping of my sowing,
I still have praise to offer up the Lord.

Like many New Testament passages
Of the blind, the bound, and the lame ,
After their healing and their deliverance ,
They went on their way with a praise.

After my near death experience,
And after I was let go from my job,
Yes there were fears and yes there were tears,
But there was also a praise for my God.

In this life there will be joy and laughter,
There will be good times and times filled with pain,
Lessons and blessings, and everything in between,
But always, always, there'll be praise.

"I will bless the LORD at all times; His praise shall continually be in my mouth."

Psalm 34:1

MY HEART'S DESIRE

Psalm 37:4-5

One day I read the promise
In Psalms 37:4
"God will give you your heart's desire,
If you delight yourself in the Lord."

Quickly I began to list
Everything my heart desired.
Then I took the list before the Lord in prayer,
And prayed down heaven's fire.

While waiting for those blessings,
Instead of giving me what I'd asked,
God led me to the following verse,
To show me how they would come to pass.

"Commit thy ways unto the Lord."
Trust in Him and Him alone.
Be delighted to do things His way,
Instead of going out on my own.

The Lord wanted me to submit
Completely unto Him,
The actions that I wanted to take,
And the motives I kept within.

He wanted me to totally surrender
Body, mind, and soul,
Depend on Him for everything,
And trust in Him alone.

Then the blessings started pouring in,
That verse the Lord fulfilled.
He gave me my heart's desires
Because I delighted in His will.

"Delight yourself also in the LORD, and He shall give you the desires of your heart. Commit your way to the LORD, Trust also in Him, And He shall bring it to pass."

Psalm 37:4-5

"YOU ARE THE DESIRE OF SOMEONE'S HEART"

Psalm 37:4-5

Often as believers we have been taught to praise God in advance for what we've asked Him for. One day in prayer I was doing just that regarding my request for a husband. My prayer was, "Lord, You said in Your word that You would give me the desires of my heart, and I believe that. I thank You now for giving me a godly husband, for that is the desire of my heart. I don't know who he is, where he is, or when he'll arrive, but I'm thanking You now for my husband."

As I continued, the Lord said to me, "YOU are the desire of someone's heart." I inquired, "I am the desire of somebody's heart? ME?" God answered back, "Someone is praying for you." I immediately began to thank and praise the Lord even more.

Then I asked Lord, "What should I do, what should I do?" In my excitement I stopped praying and started wondering who he was, how would we meet, when would we get married?

God spoke again, over all those thoughts and said, "Live your life. Live your life." Instantly a peace settled over me that was so sweet, so tangible, and so real that I began to smile. I understood what my role is in all of this. All I have to do is life my life and trust God to take care of the rest.

And that's what I've been doing ever since.

"Delight yourself in the LORD, and He will give you the desires of your heart Commit your way to the LORD, Trust in Him, and He will bring it to pass."

Psalm 37:4-5

YOU ALONE

Psalm 42:1

As the deer pants for water,
My soul pants after Thee.
My soul thirsts for You alone,
Because You set me free.

You alone, Lord Jesus Christ,
Loved me way back when,
I didn't even love myself,
So filthy I was from sin.

But You alone didn't hesitate,
To cleanse me with Your blood,
And set me in heavenly places,
I had never before dreamed of.

You alone empower me,
With Your Spirit every day.
You alone know I can't see,
And so You lead the way.

You alone fill the darkness
With the protection of Your word.
I can sleep through nights in peace,
Little voices now unheard.

You alone, Lord, You alone,
Know the joys and pains inside.
And You alone beckon me
Beneath Your wings to hide.

You alone, are my true love,
How could I want for more,
When in the spirit You sing to me
Songs I've never heard before?

You alone, Lord of my life,
I live to do Your will.
Knowing that if I seek You first,
Unspoken prayers will be fulfilled.

You alone, the Most High God,
I am Your living sacrifice,
Holy and acceptable to You alone,
My heart, my soul, my mind.

You alone, my King of kings,
And I give You all the praise,
For You alone are worthy,
Far more than words can say.

You alone, Lord, You alone,
I pledge my love to You,
Not just with these rhyming words,
But Your commandments I will do.

As the deer pants for water,
My soul pants after Thee.
My soul thirsts for You alone,
Because You set me free.

"As the deer pants for the water brooks, so pants my soul for You, O God."

Psalm 42:1

SEE JESUS
Psalm 63:2

As you come into the church building,
Whatever day it may be,
For prayer, rehearsal, or Bible class,
I hope it's Jesus that you see.

Whether Sunday morning service,
Or an afternoon service for an auxiliary,
Whether a local service, or one with guests,
I hope it's Jesus that you see.

If it's a wedding, then as you celebrate;
If it's a funeral, then as you grieve;
I hope that you realize you're in the house of God
And it's Jesus that you see.

When you're leading worship during a service
And the congregation gets quiet on you,
Don't be discouraged or deflated
Just see Jesus in every pew.

Our focus should be on Jesus,
Whether out front or behind the scenes,
We are to do everything in His name,
Whether in word or in deed.

As you're singing in the choir,
Or giving your personal testimony,
Just close your eyes and remember
"It's Jesus I'm here to see."

"So I have looked for You in the sanctuary,
To see Your power and Your glory."
Psalm 63:2

THE GREATER REFUGE

Psalm 91:1

The one found in the secret place,
Of the Most Almighty God,
Will remain under His shadow
And there he shall abide.

I will this say about the Lord:
He's my shelter and my fortress,
He alone is the only Wise God,
And in Him alone will I trust.

From traps of the evil one,
He will protect me.
And from death and disease,
He will cover me.

He will hide me with His mighty hand,
And underneath His wing,
I am safe soley because,
He shields me from everything.

Of the arrows from the devil,
Of destruction everyday,
Of the many terrors of the night,
I will not be afraid.

It doesn't matter how close trouble comes
Only with my eyes will I see,
The wrath of God towards the wicked,
No evil will come upon me.

All because I have made the Lord,
My only habitation.
My dwelling place, my resting place
My refuge and safe haven.

He even gives His angels,
Instructions every day,
To insulate and guard me,
And to keep me from harm's way.

He will be with me in trouble,
He will answer when I call.
He will bless me and honor me,
Because I love Him most of all.

He will deliver me at all times
And in every situation.
He will satisfy me with a long life,
And show me His salvation.

"He who dwells in the secret place of the Most High shall abide under the shadow of the Almighty."

Psalm 91:1

THE BARE PRAISE

Psalm 111:1

Beneath each note of music,
In every song that we sing,
Lies a melody of praise within,
That even the angels can't sing.

Between my hands lifted up in praise,
And underneath my shouting feet,
Beats a silent praise within me,
That even I can't see.

When the word of God's been spoken,
And the sermon's been said and done,
"Thy word have I hid in my heart so that
I will not sin against Your son."

Even in the midst of my prayers,
Sometimes I run out of words,
But the praises continue in my spirit,
Making intercession that can't be heard.

Even between these simple words,
Between every verse and every line,
There is a praise deep within my soul,
That has stood the test of time.

*"Praise ye the LORD. I will praise the LORD with my whole heart,
in the assembly of the upright, and in the congregation."*

Psalm 111:1

STANDING ON HIS WORD

Psalm 119:25, 50, 62, 75, 147, 165

I've come to know God by His word,
And I can truly say,
There's nothing I can't handle,
If I trust Him and obey.

I know just where to look,
No matter what I'm going through,
I've learn to heed God's Spirit,
When He directs me to read a chapter or two.

I've learn to stand upon God's word,
With each wind that Satan blows,
Whether temptations, tests, or trials,
I always know just where to go.

I even use God's word in prayer,
When I fall upon my knees,
And whenever I do, I find strength
And peace that's comforting.

So, I'm standing on the word of God,
From it I'll never depart.
It's safely tucked away and hidden,
Deep within my heart.

"My soul clings to the dust, revive me according to Your word!"
Psalm 119:25

"This is my comfort in my affliction, for Your word has given me life."
Psalm 119:50

"At midnight I rise to give thanks to You because of Your righteous word."
Psalm 119:62

"I know, O Lord, that Your word is right, and that in faithfulness You have afflicted me."
Psalm 110:75

"I rise before dawn and cry for help. I hope in your word."
Psalm 119:147

"Great peace have those who love your word, nothing can make them stumble."
Psalm 119:165

THE TREASURE MAP

Psalm 119:105

A Christian's life is sometimes called a "walk"
And as we walk each day,
We'll stay on the straight and narrow,
If we let God lead the way.

In the word of God are directions,
And instructions to get us there.
How to walk, where to walk,
And when we should beware.

The word of God - from beginning to end -
Is a road map for life,
For us to follow forward step by step,
Turning neither to the left nor the right.

"Walk uprightly for the good things in life."
"Walk in His ways and in His truth."
You'll find those passages when you take the time,
To read Psalms 84:11 and Psalm 15:2.

Isaiah 2:5 says that we should
Walk with the Lord in His light.
Ezekiel 11:20 says walk in His statutes and,
Daniel 4:37 warns against walking in pride.

Romans 6:4 says as Christ just as was buried,
From our sinful life we've died.
So we can walk in the newness of life, resurrected,
After we have been baptized into Christ.

The familiar verse of 2nd Corinthians 5:7
"Walk by faith and not by sight."
Trusting that Jesus can see way down the road,
That we travel in our life.

"Walk worthy of the your calling."
Is found in Ephesians 4:1
And Ephesians 5:2 tells us to
"Walk in the love" of the Son.

When we are in the presence of unbelievers,
Colossians 4:5 says be sure to "walk wisely."
And Revelations 21:24 promises that we shall
"Walk in the light" of that New City.

Yes, the bible is a spiritual road map,
And if we follow it, we'll find,
A special treasure in the end,
Buried in the sky.

"Your word is a lamp to my feet and a light to my path."
Psalm 119:105

WITH MY WHOLE HEART

Psalm 119:133

Teach me oh Lord,
Right now, I want to start,
By obeying Your statutes,
With my whole heart.

Teach me oh Lord,
And never again will I depart,
From cherishing Your word,
With my whole heart.

Teach me oh Lord,
To quench each wicked fiery dart,
With faith in Your word,
With my whole heart.

Teach me oh Lord,
To be conscious of every idle remark,
And to endeavor to please You,
With my whole heart.

Teach me oh Lord,
To rightly take your word apart,
And spiritually apply it to my life,
With my whole heart.

Teach me oh Lord,
These words I do impart,
Because I want to live for you,
With my whole heart.

"Teach me, O LORD, the way of thy statutes; and I shall keep it unto the end."
Psalm 119:133

GOD IS STANDING IN-BETWEEN

Psalm 139:7-12

Throughout the ups and downs of life,
God is standing in-between.
As a healer, deliverer and Savior,
On which we can always lean.

But God is also standing in-between
Us and the bad decisions we make.
When we willfully choose to sin,
When we wallow in bitterness and hate.

God is standing in-between
The gossiping words we say,
The ttale bearing we take part in
When news of a scandal comes our way.

God is standing in-between,
In fact he's right in front of our face,
When we see that person we just can't stand,
And we roll our eyes in distaste.

God is standing in-between
The hurt we cause one another,
Believe it or not it hurts him too
When there's dissenion among sisters and brothers.

We think that we're in good standing with God,
Because He wakes us up each dawn.
But He is standing in-between
The sin that lingers on.

Just because we sing and shout
Doesn't mean our sin is unknown,
He is a patient and loving God
But we will reap what we have sown.

When this life is over
And from this world we take our leave,
We'll discover that when it comes to heaven and hell
God is still standing in-between.

"Where can I go from Your Spirit? or where can I flee from Your presence?
If I ascend into heaven, You are there; if I make my bed in hell, behold, You are there.
If I take the wings of the morning, and dwell in the uttermost parts of the sea,
Even there Your hand shall lead me, and Your right hand shall hold me.
If I say, "Surely the darkness shall fall on me," even the night shall be light about me;
Indeed, the darkness shall not hide from You, but the night shines as the day;
The darkness and the light are both alike to You."
Psalm 139:7-12

YES, I'M JUST THAT GREAT

Psalm 145:3

As the praise team began to sing,
"How Great is Our God"
I closed my eyes in worship,
And began to sing along.

Faces came before me,
Hearts and homes in pain,
And as they did, I heard God say,
"Yes, I'm just that Great.

"I'm great enough to mend fences,
That seem permanently destroyed.
I'm great enough to transform,
Turmoil into joy.

"I'm great enough to heal any sickness,
And give grace enough to endure.
I'm great enough to change secret agendas,
Into motives sincere and pure."

So whatever you are going through,
Just whisper a prayer of praise,
Secure in the knowledge that no matter what,
Our God is just that great.

"Great is the LORD, and greatly to be praised; And His greatness is unsearchable."

Psalm 145:3

PROVERBS

FIRST FRUITS

Proverbs 3:9-10 | Malachi 3:10

If you honor the Lord with your substance,
By freely giving of your increase,
Then your barrels will burst forth with new wine,
And your barns will be filled with plenty.

But if you keep your to yourself,
And refuse to open your purse,
In essence you are robbing God,
And for that you will be cursed.

So bring all your tithes into God's house,
Prove God's word and see,
He'll pour out so many blessings,
You won't have room enough to receive.

God will rebuke the enemy for your sake,
And give you the strength to stand.
All mankind will call you blessed,
Yours will be a delightful land.

"Honor the LORD with your possessions, And with the first fruits of all your increase; So your barns will be filled with plenty, And your vats will overflow with new wine."

Proverbs 3:9-10

"Bring the full tithe into the storehouse, that there may be food in my house. And thereby put me to the test, says the LORD of hosts, if I will not open the windows of heaven for you and pour down for you a blessing until there is no more need."

Malachi 3:8

THE CATCH OF THE DAY

Proverbs 11:30b | Matthew 4:19

Before you clean a fish,
You've got to catch it first.
You've got to be like a good fisherman.
You've got to use the best of worms.

You can't rush out on the dock,
And just throw in the bait.
You've got to approach slowly,
Gently toss in the line and wait.

And while you're waiting, you must be still,
And as quiet as can be,
And when you feel a little tug,
Don't start screaming happily.

You might lose the catch when you reel it in,
If your celebration is premature.
So instead you should be calm,
Steady, and very sure.

Once you do reel it in,
And the fish is wiggling at the end of the line,
A few moments from final surrender,
Yet still refusing to give up the fight.

Resist the urge to take the hook out,
Because he'll squirm all over the deck.
You know how fish are out of water,
They're bound to jump right back in.

You must wait until it surrenders,
Then let the celebration begin.
Gently scrape the scales off its body,
And carefully remove each fin.

And so it is with all of us,
For didn't Jesus say,
"Follow me and I'll make you fishers of men"?
Well that still applies to us today.

And as we fish out souls for Christ,
We must be very sure,
That the soul is Holy Ghost hooked,
We can't afford to be premature.

We can't go out on the docks of this world,
Making a lot of noise,
We've got to be gentle, kind, and calm,
Full of compassion and poise.

We've got to be sure of the bait we use,
And the best bait we can find,
Is the word of God, for then they'll be,
Sure to tug that line.

And when we feel their line start to pull,
And see their interest grow,
We can't be too quick to reel them in,
We've got to take it slow.

Because just like fish, if you pull a person too hard,
You're bound to shake them loose.
You're pulling this way, the world is pulling that way,
And they're not sure yet which road to choose.

The best thing to do is to wait patiently,
They'll come of their own accord.
Jesus will draw in that line,
If we just lift up the name of the Lord.

The word of God clearly says,
"He that wins souls is wise."
Let God truly catch the soul before
We try to doctrinalize.

Then after all is said and done,
We won't say *"That's the one that got away."*
Instead, each and every soul that's caught,
Will be called "The catch of the day."

"He who wins souls is wise."
Proverbs 11:30b

"Then He said to them, 'Follow Me, and I will make you fishers of men'."
Matthew 4:19

A REAL MAN OF GOD
Proverbs 24:16a

He's not perfect like Christ Jesus,
Though he really strives to be.
He's more like Peter and Thomas,
Sometimes he has doubts and unbelief.

He's not an angel sent from heaven,
No, he's still living in the flesh.
But like David when confronted with his sin,
This man will truly repent.

He's not under the anointing,
Twenty four hours of the day.
He's more like Jonah, he'll do the Lord's will,
Though at first he may try to stray.

He doesn't possess the strength of Samson,
Or the wisdom of Solomon.
But like them both, he'll have the victory,
When all is said and done.

He may not have the courage of Joshua,
Or be as anointed as Apostle Paul.
But this man with all his frailties,
Still considers Christ his all.

For a just man falleth seven times, and riseth up again:
Proverbs 24:16a

THE VIRTUOUS WOMAN
Proverbs 31:10

She's worth far more than rubies.
She's as precious as fine gold.
She's not ashamed of the gospel of Christ
She stands firm, and sure, and bold.

She is truly a virtuous woman,
You hear wisdom when she speaks.
Her tongue is always full of kindness,
Gentleness and peace.

She helps the poor and needy,
Honor and strength is how she's dressed,
She works willingly with her hands,
Even her children call her blessed.

She is an example to all women,
Rising early and working late,
Other women have done good works,
But she exceeds them in every way.

A woman of favor can be deceitful,
And a woman of beauty is sometimes vain,
But a virtuous woman reverences and fears the Lord,
And her works will bring her praise.

"Who can find a virtuous wife? For her worth is far above rubies."

Proverbs 31:10

ECCLESIASTES

KEEP UP THE STANDARDS

Ecclesiastes 12:1

[Written for the Greater Refuge Graduation Scholarship Banquet]

Years ago I was one of you, and someone said to me:
"Keep up the standards no matter what, or you will be sorry."

What they meant by standards were the principles and rules,
That I'd been taught to live by, at home, in church, and school.

Where each of you are right now, I remember being there,
And I took those standards lightly, without a thought or care.

My whole life was in front of me, but I let my standards slip away.
Everything I learned went out the window, and I learned the hard way.

I learned with every tear I shed, and every year that passed,
With every broken standard, and with every failed test.

With every missed opportunity, and every shattered dream,
I learned that keeping my standards, was more serious than it seemed.

You will hear people tell you, "You're young, go ahead, have fun!"
But I am here to tell you life is not a game, and life is almost done.

I say that because Jesus is coming back, and He's coming back to find,
Those who kept the standards, and kept them all the time.

So keep up the standards of always seeking God in prayer,
Don't be ashamed of the gospel of Christ, stand up for it anywhere.

Keep up the standard of obeying God's holy word,
Remember that pleasing God is better than doing what you prefer.

Keep up the standards that you've learned, don't change for anyone.
And believe me folks will try their best to undo what God has done.

The world will test your standards to see how strong you really are.
Your dearest friends will challenge you, and so will strangers from afar.

Keep up all the standards, of what you learn in school.
Getting good grades will take you farther than being popular or cool.

Keep up all the standards of what you learned in church.
God has plans for each of you to be a special part of His work.

Keep up the standards and be sure to keep off the streets.
Try to live the things you've learned, practice what's been preached.

So keep up all the standards, no matter how hard it seems.
Salvation and education - you can reach God and your dreams!

"Remember now your Creator in the days of your youth,
Before the difficult days come, and the years draw near when you say,
'I have no pleasure in them'."

Ecclesiastes 12:1

SONG OF SOLOMON

I WILL SING

Song of Solomon 2:11-12

Early one summer morning,
Before the sun began to rise,
The clouds opened up in the heavens,
And rain poured down from the skies.

Thunder smacked, crackled and popped,
So loud it shook me awake.
I opened my eyes just in time to see,
Lightening strike across time and space.

As I lay in my bed in the darkness,
Listening to this summer storm.
I tried my best to forget that I ,
Was going through a storm of my own.

In the distance, beyond all the thunder,
In the midst of the storm and the rain,
I heard a sound that made me smile,
Birds were chirping their songs of praise.

Though the rain beat down upon them,
Though the lightning flashed across their skies,
Though the sound of thunder was deafening,
It didn't stop me from hearing their cries.

Sweet sounding cries of birds rejoicing,
With songs to their Creator and King.
A lesson that even though it's raining in my life,
My soul should continue to sing.

For my Creator is still deserving,
To hear my own song of praise.
It's the reason He created me,
It's the reason He woke me up that day.

"For, lo, the winter is past, the rain is over and gone;
The flowers appear on the earth; the time of the singing of birds is come."

Song of Solomon 2:11-12

Isaiah

HERE AM I, SEND ME

Isaiah 6:6-9

Like Isaiah, I prayed to the Lord,
Here am I, Lord, please send me.
If You need a willing worker,
I'm just the servant for Thee.

I will warn your people,
I will speak of what's to come,
I will let them know what saith the Lord
That Your kingdom is surely come.

But before You send me out to do this,
There's something You must do,
Before I can minister to your people,
I must be cleansed through and through.

Whether hot coals upon my lips,
Or cloven tongues of fire from on high,
Let the power of Your holy spirit,
Baptize me with Your fire.

For I recognize my sinful nature,
Against Your divine holiness,
And my need for continuous renewal,
Before I fulfill Your request.

Wherever you may lead me
Mountains high or valleys low,
Good times or trying times,
Send me, Lord, I'll go.

Through the fire, I won't be burned,
Just like Shadrak, Meeshak, and Abednego.
That same figure that looked like the Son of God,
Will be with me wherever I go.

If I go through the floods, they won't overtake me,
Because the Lord has anchored my soul,
The waves may splash, but I will still proclaim,
Send me, Lord, I'll go.

Experience has taught me,
To go wherever You lead,
Regardless of my own will,
It is You I aim to please.

"I heard the voice of the Lord, saying:
'Whom shall I send, and who will go for Us?'
Then I said, 'Here am I! Send me'."

Isaiah 6:9

SEND YOUR ANOINTING

Isaiah 10:27

Anointing is another word for oil, or fat
So what this scripture really means,
Is when the oxen are fed, their necks enlarge,
And their yokes break away from the seams.

In the same manner, when we are filled
With God's anointing – His spirit and His word,
Then the sinful, demonic yokes that have us bound
Will ultimately be destroyed.

Lord, lift the burdens from Your people,
Destroy the weights and burdens we bear.
The only thing that can bring us relief
Is if You send Your anointing here.

Let Your anointing, which is Your Holy Spirit
Destroy the yokes that fill our minds,
Attacks by the enemy of our souls,
Designed to separate us from Christ.

Let Your anointing destroy the yokes in our homes,
Evil spirits here and there,
Sent to tempt us and to taunt us,
Sent to cause us doubts and fears.

Let it destroy the yokes in our mouths,
The hurtful, sinful words we say,
Let Your anointing, which is Your love
Flavor our words throughout each day.

Let Your anointing, which is Your presence
Search deep within our hearts,
Apply the blood of Jesus,
And let all wickedness depart.

For only Your anointing
Can give us sweet release,
From the chains that try to bind us,
And take our focus off of Thee.

Lord please send Your anointing,
There is so much work for us to do.
We can be free to accomplish Your will,
If You send Your anointing, which is You.

"It shall come to pass in that day that his burden will be taken away
from your shoulder, and his yoke from your neck,
and the yoke will be destroyed because of the anointing oil."

Isaiah 10:27

"I AM HERE"
Isaiah 41:9-10,13

I was going through a financial crisis and I didn't know what to do, where to go, and who to ask for help. I began to suffer from insomnia and depression, not to mention guilt. The scripture in Psalm 42:3, *"My tears have been my meat day and night,"* became my reality. I was tortured with the fear of losing everything. I covered all of this up with a nonchalant attitude and curt responses to anyone who dared ask me what was wrong.

This was the condition I was in on that Sunday as morning service ended and the congregation began to set up for communion. Inside, I felt lost, alone, afraid. I just didn't see a way out of the financial trouble I was in. To all of the saints sitting in my vicinity I loudly announced, *"I am not taking communion. I'm going home."* I told my children, *"Get ready. We're leaving."* They got their belongings together and headed towards the foyer of the church. I stood up, gathered my things, heading out as well, but for some reason my feet walked across the front of the sanctuary, through the chapel, and down the hallway towards the prayer room.

As soon as I stepped through the door, I collapsed onto the floor and, burst into tears. I started saying *"Help me, help me,"* over and over. I told God that I was afraid. I asked Him what should I do. After some minutes, I heard He so clearly and so lovingly to me. He only said three words: "I am here." Instantly, I felt peace. Instantly, I felt relief. Instantly, I felt joy. I stayed there a little while longer telling Him I was sorry for my anger. Then got up, went to find my children, and we made our way home.

God didn't give me any answers that Sunday. I didn't receive an unexpected check in the mail the next day that made everything all right. Nobody called me with a perfect solution to my dilemma. But I was at peace and I felt full of joy simply because God told me He was there. And knowing that meant that I would be alright. Everything would be alright, because God was with me.

About five weeks later, my situation changed and just like I thought, things did get better. My children and I were alright. Truly, the Lord was with us.

"You are My servant, I have chosen you and have not cast you away:
Fear not, for I am with you; Be not dismayed, for I am your God.
I will strengthen you, Yes, I will help you,
I will uphold you with My righteous right hand.'
For I, the LORD your God, will hold your right hand,
Saying to you, 'Fear not, I will help you'."

Isaiah 41:9-10, 13

MY NAME IS NOT MOTHER NATURE

Isaiah 42:8

I am the Alpha and Omega,
The beginning and the end,
The first and the last.
My name is not Mother Nature,
 I am the Lord – That is My name!

I am the Wonderful Counselor,
The Mighty God, The Everlasting Father,
And the Prince of Peace.
My name is not Mother Nature,
 I am the Lord – That is My name!

I am the Lilly of the Valley,
The Bright and Morning Star,
The Stone hued out of Jesse.
My name is not Mother Nature,
 I am the Lord – That is My name!

I am that I Am,
I am The Holy One,
Who is and was and is to come.
The Word made flesh,
And manifested into the Son.
I am God – My Father and I are one.
My name is not Mother Nature,
 I AM THE LORD – THAT IS MY NAME!

*"I am the LORD, that is My name; I will not give My glory to another,
Nor My praise to graven images."*

Isaiah 42:8

RUSHING BACK TO ME

Isaiah 55:11

In my hour of fear and loneliness,
Your word comes rushing back to me,
And I remember Joseph:
How through no fault of his own,
He was betrayed, falsely accused, and imprisoned.
But it worked out for his good and Your glory,
Because to save much people alive
Was the moral of his story.

In my hour of sickness and shame,
Your word comes rushing back to me,
And I remember Job:
How after he lost everything -
Possessions, family, friends, and his good health -
He never cursed Your sovereignty.
And when all was said and done,
In his latter days, he won.

In my hour of sin and failure,
Your word comes rushing back to me,
And I remember David:
How after his sin of adultery and murder
In guilt and shame, he truly repented,
Never to do those things again,
And never ceasing afterwards
To give Your name the praise.

In my hour of feeling overwhelmed,
Your word comes rushing back to me,
And I see you in Gethsemane:
In Your hour of humanity,
You willingly faced Calvary,
Your "Nevertheless" was just for me,
So that no matter what this life may bring,
I can overcome triumphantly.

"For as the rain cometh down, and the snow from heaven,
and returneth not thither, but watereth the earth,
and maketh it bring forth and bud,
that it may give seed to the sower, and bread to the eater:
So shall My word be that goes forth from My mouth;
It shall not return to Me void, But it shall accomplish what I please,
And it shall prosper in the thing for which I sent it."

Isaiah 55:10-11

JEREMIAH

RETURN OH BACKSLIDER

Jeremiah 3:12-14

When we hear the word backslider,
A stereotype comes to mind,
Of someone so full of sin,
They left the church behind.

But the word backslider simply means
Someone who slid back,
Whether for a moment or forever,
They're spiritually off track.

In the book of Jeremiah
God speaks to those who left,
And His love for backsliding Israel,
Exemplifies His love for us.

He says:

"Return to me, oh backslider,
Confess what you have done.
Forsake the desire to do it again,
And just come on back home.

"Return to me, my precious child,
Admit in prayer your sin.
I'll forgive you and restore you,
If you've repented deep within.

"Come back to Me in the spirit,
And I'll forgive your wickedness.
I'll fill you with the strength you need,
To pass each tempting test.

"Come back to me, come back to me,
I love you like a wife.
I'll forgive all of your adulterous ways,
And give our love new life.

"Return to me, my love, because
I am still married to you.
I will still extend my mercy,
If you're sorry through and through.

"For when you slipped away from me,
And from the center of my will,
You chose worldly pleasures
Over the promises I can fulfill.

"But I will take you back, dear one,
And love you all the more.
I'll root you and ground you in My word,
So you won't stray like before."

Oh backslider, God is calling you
With every hour you live through.
He's calling you with every breath you take,
And every morning you wake up to.

Oh backslider, God is even calling you
Throught the words of this poetry.
He wanted me to tell you that He said,
"Backslider, return to Me."

He doesn't care if you've been gone for years,
Or only for a few days.
He wants you to fall upon your knees,
And ask Him your soul to save.

"'Return, backsliding Israel,' says the LORD; 'I will not cause My anger to fall on you. For I am merciful,' says the LORD; 'I will not remain angry forever. 'Return, O backsliding children,' says the LORD; 'for I am married to you'."

Jeremiah 3:12,14

THE PASTOR AFTER
Jeremiah 3:15

[Written and dedicated to my former pastor, District Elder M. E. Jones]

We praise God for giving us
A pastor just like you,
Who not only teaches us His word,
But lives and obeys it too.

We thank God for how you minister,
To the natural and spiritual man,
With everyday examples
That even the youth understand.

We're blessed because of your humbleness
And the way you're always there,
To confide in, to counsel, to laugh with
And to remember us in prayer.

We love you and we honor you
You're a pastor after God's own heart.
So when you ask, "Are you with me?"
Our answer is "Yes we are!"

*"And I will give you pastors according to mine heart,
which shall feed you with knowledge and understanding."*

Jeremiah 3:15

GOD OF ALL

Jeremiah 32:26-27

Moses parted the Red Sea,
With that powerful rod.
He made the river Jordan
Stand back by the power of God.

When David was a young man,
Strong and defiant,
He used a stone and a sling,
To kill Goliath the giant.

The three Hebrew boys,
Shadrach, Meshach and Abednego,
Were delivered from a fiery furnace
So very long ago.

Mary, while still a virgin,
Was engaged to be Joseph's wife,
Through the power of God alone,
She gave birth to Jesus Christ.

The disciples that were chosen,
To follow Jesus by faith,
They witnessed Him save, heal, and deliver,
The deaf, the blind, the lame.

The Sadducees and Pharisees
Refused to just believe
But when Jesus rose they realized,
That He was God's Son indeed.

Those in the upper room,
On that first Pentecostal day,
Heard a messaged preached by Peter
"Repent and be baptized in Jesus' name."

John was given a revelation,
And through God He prophesied,
The ending of this very world,
And the second coming of Jesus Christ.

All of this and more was written
So very long ago,
So that we would have faith in God
And so we would always know:

That regardless of any circumstance, sickness,
Enemy, element, or sin,
He is the God of all flesh,
There is nothing too hard for Him.

"Then the word of the LORD came to Jeremiah, saying,
'Behold, I am the LORD, the God of all flesh.
Is there anything too hard for Me?'"

Jeremiah 32:26-27

LAMENTATIONS

THE WAY THAT GOD SEES ME

Lamentations 3:40-41

I used my eyes as windows to judge others,
Until God made me see,
Myself through His eyes,
And what I saw startled me.

I saw myself as I was in sin,
Then I saw the blood applied.
I saw myself at the altar where,
Reclaimed, to sin I died.

I saw the times since then that I,
Found myself out of God's will.
I saw the way His word stood true,
"Confess, and He'll forgive."

I see the way, even up to this day,
I still fall short of God's glory,
Yet His grace and mercy still allow,
Me to share with you my story.

In all of this, I see God's love,
Unfailing, unfaltering, and true.
In all of my unworthiness,
Everyday, His mercies are new.

God made me use my eyes as a mirror,
He made me see deep inside,
My heart and soul and I have found,
That within me He does abide.

And because of this, I've learned to use
My heart, others to see,
With understanding and compassion,
The way that God sees me.

"Let us search out and examine our ways and turn back to the LORD;
Let us lift our hearts and hands to God in heaven."

Lamentations 3:40-41

EZEKIEL

THE WATCHMAN

Ezekiel 33:6

God has set up watchman,
To whom He'll give a sign,
To warn folks of the day,
When the sword is going to strike.

God has set a watchman,
(Maybe more than one),
To blow the trumpet as a signal,
That the end has surely come.

Now if the watchman warns the people,
And they fail to take heed,
When the sword comes against them,
They will die in iniquity.

Their blood will be upon their own hands,
They will have no one to blame.
The watchman did his duty,
And his own soul will be saved.

But if the watchman hears from God,
And fails to let the people know,
And if the sword comes against them,
And they aren't prepared to go;

They'll still be held accountable,
For their individual sin,
But their blood will be required by God
At the hands of the watchman.

So, if God has set you as a watchman,
And told you the sword is on its way,
Warn the people, sound the trumpet,
So God's wrath you will escape.

"But if the watchman sees the sword coming and does not blow the trumpet,
and the people are not warned, and the sword comes and takes any person
from among them, he is taken away in his iniquity; but his blood
I will require at the watchman's hand."

Ezekiel 33:6

Poems & Testimonies Inspired by the New Testament

"For the word of God is living and powerful, and sharper than any two-edged sword, piercing even to the division of soul and spirit, and of joints and marrow, and is a discerner of the thoughts and intents of the heart."

Hebrews 4:12

MATTHEW

A JOURNEY OF FAITH

Matthew 1:19-24; 2:13-15; 19-23

Between the lines of the Christmas story,
Is a message of love and faith,
That show no matter what the situation,
God will surely lead and guide the way.

There's one central message,
And of course it's all about love.
God had so much of it for this word,
Left His heavenly home above.

Wrapped himself in flesh,
To save all of humanity,
But before He was born of a virgin,
He tested the depths of Josep's belief.

The big picture was all about purpose,
That's why every move he made,
Rested on his ability to live,
With his God and his family by faith.

Joseph's relationship was tested first,
His trust in Mary was paramount,
He was understandably skepital
Until he heard the angel's account.

Joseph was tested in his ability,
To truly hear God's voice,
In spite of all the others,
That may have questioned his choice.

Joseph's faith in God was tried in the fire,
And he turned out to be,
And man who knew how to discern God's will,
A man of integrity.

Every step in Joseph's journey,
Proved he had faith in God's divine plan,
He knew that Jesus was precious cargo,
Sent to save the soul of man.

"Then Joseph her husband, being a just man, and not wanting to make her a public example, was minded to put her away secretly. But while he thought about these things, behold, an angel of the Lord appeared to him in a dream, saying, "Joseph, son of David, do not be afraid to take to you Mary your wife, for that which is conceived in her is of the Holy Spirit. And she will bring forth a Son, and you shall call His name JESUS, for He will save His people from their sins." So all this was done that it might be fulfilled which was spoken by the Lord through the prophet, saying: "Behold, the virgin shall be with child, and bear a Son, and they shall call His name Immanuel," which is translated, "God with us." Joseph, being aroused from sleep, did as the angel of the Lord commanded him and took to him his wife, and did not know her till she had brought forth her firstborn Son. And he called His name JESUS."

Matthew 1:19-24

"Now when they had departed, behold, an angel of the Lord appeared to Joseph in a dream, saying, "Arise, take the young Child and His mother, flee to Egypt, and stay there until I bring you word; for Herod will seek the young Child to destroy Him." When he arose, he took the young Child and His mother by night and departed for Egypt, and was there until the death of Herod, that it might be fulfilled which was spoken by the Lord through the prophet, saying, 'Out of Egypt I called My Son.'"

Matthew 2:13-15

"Now when Herod was dead, behold, an angel of the Lord appeared in a dream to Joseph in Egypt, saying, "Arise, take the young Child and His mother, and go to the land of Israel, for those who sought the young Child's life are dead." Then he arose, took the young Child and His mother, and came into the land of Israel. But when he heard that Archelaus was reigning over Judea instead of his father Herod, he was afraid to go there. And being warned by God in a dream, he turned aside into the region of Galilee. And he came and dwelt in a city called Nazareth, that it might be fulfilled which was spoken by the prophets, 'He shall be called a Nazarene.'"

Matthew 2:19-23

WE ALL KNOW
Matthew 1:23

[Written and recited for Bell Atlantic's annual Christmas office party]

We all know the real meaning of Christmas,
Is not Santa coming down the chimney,
Or how many gifts our children find,
Under the Christmas tree.

We all know the biblical story,
Of Mary, Joseph, the wise men,
And Jesus, who was born in a manger,
Because their was no room in the inn.

And most of us also know that,
The Christmas story doesn't stop there,
For baby Jesus grew up to be,
Much more than He first appeared.

To Joseph and Mary Jesus was,
Their miracle baby, special and beloved.
To the wise men, He was the promised Messiah,
Old Testament prophets spoke of.

To Government officials he became a threat,
Because people stopped believing in them,
And instead they looked to Jesus Christ,
And put their faith in Him.

To the deaf, dumb, and to the blind,
Jesus turned out to be,
A doctor with all healing power,
He could even cure leprosy.

To the rich who didn't think they needed anything,
Jesus simply became a friend,
He promised never to forsake them,
And to stick with them until the end.

To people in general Jesus became a Savior,
And whatever they needed saving from.
They looked to Him for guidance,
Because they knew He was God's son.

Yes, the Christmas story spans a lifetime,
And after that life came to an end,
Jesus showed up alive and kicking,
Living in the heart and minds of men.

So, what do you want for Christmas?
What's missing in your life?
Not material things, like clothes or toys,
Or personal things, like a husband or a wife.

But, what do you *need* this Christmas?
What void do you want filled?
Nothing else will satisfy you,
Like the love of Jesus will.

The love that Jesus has for you,
Isn't under a Christmas tree,
It's in the cross He hung from,
When He died at Calvary.

It's in the words of the bible,
And it's deep within the heart,
Of others who have already received,
The love He wants to impart.

You don't have to wait until Christmas,
To get this gift Christ has for you,
He'll give it when you ask in faith,
And with a heart's that's true.

"Therefore, the Lord Himself will give you a sign: Behold,
a virgin shall conceive and bear a Son, and shall call His name Immanuel."

"For unto us a Child is born, unto us a Son is given; And the government will be upon His shoulder. And His name will be called Wonderful, Counselor, Mighty God, Everlasting Father, Prince of Peace. Of the increase of His government and peace there will be no end, Upon the throne of David and over His kingdom, To order it and establish it with judgment and justice From that time forward, even forever. The zeal of the LORD of hosts will perform this."

Isaiah 7:14; 9:6-7

"Behold, the virgin shall be with child, and bear a Son,
and they shall call His name Immanuel," which is translated, 'God with us.'"

Matthew 1:23

A HUNGER FOR CHRIST

Matthew 5:6

All around this world today,
People are hungry for many things.
Some are hungry for success,
And the power that it brings.

A few thirst for knowledge,
And a better education,
Sure that will guarantee security,
In wealthy corporations.

There are literally those who'd give their lives,
For civil rights and equality.
Others who are imprisoned behind stone walls
Longing to be free.

There are young girls hungry for love and affection,
That was missing when they were young.
And young boys itching to prove their manhood,
Thinking they've found it packing a gun.

People in this world are hungry,
They have voids that they want filled.
Empty places in empty faces,
They just don't that God is real.

"Lord give them a hungry heart.
Let them long to do Your will.
Tell them if they seek You first,
Their hearts' desire You will fulfill.

"Give them a longing deep within themselves,
For the love of Jesus Christ.
Teach them to seek You in their youth,
Instead of rushing to seek a husband or a wife.

"Grant them an appetite for Your anointing,
And a desire to fast and pray.
Awaken a need within them,
To read Your word each day."

Amen.

"Blessed are those who hunger and thirst for righteousness, for they shall be filled."
Matthew 5:6

LOVE YOUR ENEMIES

Matthew 5:44

Bless those who curse you.
Let each unkind word they say,
Be another reason to remember them,
Whenever you kneel to pray.

Do good to those who hate you,
Remember you want to be like Christ,
Who asked God to forgive the ones,
Who sought and took His life.

Pray for those who use you,
And for those who persecute you, too.
You'll find that while you're praying for them,
God will bless and strengthen you.

When you have received kindness
It's easy to give it in return
But showing it when you've been mistreated
Is the lesson Christ wants us to learn.

"You have heard that it was said, 'You shall love your neighbor and hate your enemy.' But I say to you, love your enemies, bless those who curse you, do good to those who hate you, and pray for those who spitefully use you and persecute you, that you may be sons of your Father in heaven; for He makes His sun rise on the evil and on the good, and sends rain on the just and on the unjust. For if you love those who love you, what reward have you? Do not even the tax collectors do the same? And if you greet your brethren only, what do you do more than others? Do not even the tax collectors do so? Therefore you shall be perfect, just as your Father in heaven is perfect."

Matthew 5:43-48

FORGIVE US OUR DEBTS

Matthew 6:12; 18:21

Our Father up in heaven,
Hallelujah to thy name!
I can tell Thy Kingdom is soon to come,
By these last and evil days.

Lord, I pray Your will be done,
In heaven and on earth.
I thank You for my daily bread,
I realize its worth.

And Lord, I know You will forgive,
My debts, trespasses, and wrong.
I'm sorry Father for my sins,
I know where I belong.

What was that, Lord? What did You just say?
My sins you won't forgive?
Why, I've never heard of such a thing
As long as I have lived!

Let me pause for just a moment,
At this point in my prayer,
And allow You to explain,
I think that's only fair.

Selah.

Oh, now I think I understand,
The error of my ways.
I still haven't forgiven you-know-who
For our blow up the other day.

And I must not leave out that family incident,
That happened a few years ago,
We still don't speak to this day,
But I act like I don't know.

And every time I lay eyes on
That certain old friend of mine,
My eyeballs roll upward
As if I was suddenly blind.

But You have brought to my attention
What's recorded in Your word"
"Forgive us ***as we forgive*** *others."*
What a lesson I have learned!

And now I remember that parable,
About the servant and his Lord.
He was forgiven, but he would not forgive
And found himself behind a prison door.

Father, Your word clearly says
That You will do the same to me,
If I refuse to truly forgive,
And harbor feelings of animosity .

You said 70 times 70 (or, to infinity)
That's the principle of "forgive and forget."
How I forgive others is how You'll forgive me.
Okay, Lord, now I think I'm set.

Our Father up in heaven,
Please search within my heart,
Please try my most innermost thoughts,
And let all wickedness depart.

Please fill me with a true desire
To always obey Your word.
I don't want iniquity within my heart
For then my prayers will not be heard.

Lord, from all temptations,
And all evil deliver me.
I started this prayer with my blinders on,
But now, Lord, I can see.

I end this prayer knowing what I must do
Before I ask You to foegie me again.
For Thine is the kingdom, power, and glory,
Forever and ever, Amen.

"And forgive us our debts, as we forgive our debtors."

Matthew 6:12

"So My heavenly Father also will do to you if each of you, from his heart, does not forgive his brother his trespasses."

Matthew 18:21

FIRST THINGS FIRST

Matthew 6:25-34

The Sunday morning you decide
To catch up on your sleep,
Was the Sunday that the morning message
Would have helped you get through the week.

When Bible class rolls around
You always have other plans.
Then you wonder why so much of the bible
You don't seem to understand.

God only knows the number of times
You chose to stay at home
Were the same times that the Spirit fell
On each and every one.

How about the time you missed a whole revival?
You said, "Oh, I've heard that preacher before."
Then tests and trials got you so bad you cried
"Lord, I just can't take it anymore!"

Many times you say you're busy,
You've got something else to do,
Not realizing that's the same moment,
God was planning your breakthrough.

"Seek ye first the kingdom of God
And all his righteousness."
And as for what to eat and drink ,
God said He'd add to the rest.

These things are for our spiritual needs:
Revivals, prayer, and Bible class.
Regardless of what our weekly routine may be,
Only what we do for Christ will last.

God wants the first fruits of our everything,
Not just our money but also our time/
He wants our schedules, plans and appointments,
Just as much as our hearts and our minds.

We should clear out our entire calendar,
And fill it up with Jesus first.
And use the time left over for,
Family, friends, fun and work.

"Therefore I say to you, do not worry about your life, what you will eat or what you will drink; nor about your body, what you will put on. Is not life more than food and the body more than clothing? Look at the birds of the air, for they neither sow nor reap nor gather into barns; yet your heavenly Father feeds them. Are you not of more value than they? Which of you by worrying can add one cubit to his stature? So why do you worry about clothing? Consider the lilies of the field, how they grow: they neither toil nor spin; and yet I say to you that even Solomon in all his glory was not arrayed like one of these. Now if God so clothes the grass of the field, which today is, and tomorrow is thrown into the oven, will He not much more clothe you, O you of little faith? "Therefore do not worry, saying, 'What shall we eat?' or ' What shall we drink?' or 'What shall we wear?' For after all these things the Gentiles seek. For your heavenly Father knows that you need all these things. But seek first the kingdom of God and His righteousness, and all these things shall be added to you. Therefore do not worry about tomorrow, for tomorrow will worry about its own things. Sufficient for the day is its own trouble.

Matthew 6:25:34

A(SK) S(EEK) K(NOCK)
Matthew 7:7

God broke something down to me,
Just the other day.
That helped me to fully understand,
How to really seek His face.

"**A**sk and it shall be given,
Seek and ye shall find,
Knock and the door shall be opened."
We quote this scripture all the time.

But how can you ask Him for anything,
Without seeking and finding Him first?
And how will you find Him without knocking
And waiting for Him let you in?

God took me on a spiritual journey,
And taught me how to seek His face.
How to look for Him in the spirit.
How to find Him in the midst of my praise.

He first taught me the principle of knocking,
Before asking for anything in prayer.
It's praising my way in the spirit,
And listening to make sure that He's there.

Once I've knocked my way into His presence,
The next step is to seek His face,
Then and only then will I find Him,
For He dwells in the midst of my praise.

If we keep on knocking and seeking,
We can be sure of this one thing,
Sooner or later He will show up,
And this is what He will bring:

His powerful Holy spirit,
Joy that only comes from Him,
And a sweet and pleasant anointing,
That will fill us to the very brim.

After all of our knocking and praising,
After we have sought and found His face,
Then and only then are we ready,
To ask what we will in His name.

"Ask, and it will be given to you; seek, and you will find; knock and it will be opened to you."

Matthew 7:7

ETERNITY
Matthew 7:22-23

God recently showed me a vision,
That I hope to make you see.
And the best way I can do it
Is through this poetry.

Imagine a line of people that stretches
As far as the eye can see.
Everyone is waiting to see where they
Will spend eternity.

Imagine a great throne made of gold
And on it sits the Lord.
Next to the throne is an angel
Standing in front of a door.

On the door in big bold letters are
E-T-E-R-N-I-T-Y.
And all of the people in line
Are waiting to go inside.

Now imagine out of all the people waiting,
You can only see the first four in line.
Although there are many others
They represent the millions standing behind.

Three of the four people
Are laughing and talking with glee.
One loudly says, *"Girl, I just can't wait*
To walk through that door marked Eternity!"

"I worked so hard and I waited so long.
Do you know how tough it's been
Coming to church every Sunday?
I know that angel's gonna let me in!"

Another says, *"Remember how in Jesus name*
I cast demons out of women and men?
And how I prophesied things that were to come?
I'm sure that angel's gonna let me in!"

The third one said, *"I did so many good works.*
I always gave more than ten percent!
I gave food, clothing, and my precious time.
That angel better let me in!"

On and on they chatted,
While the fourth one said to himself,
"I didn't do any great things like them."
The more they talked, the worse he felt.

Finally, the Lord began calling out names,
The first person stepped into view,
Saying *"Lord, Lord"* toward the throne,
But the Lord said, *"Who are you?"*

"Wait, wait, there must be some mistake!"
She desperately began to shout.
Out of nowhere, another angel appeared,
And escorted that first person out.

"There are no mistakes up here,"
Number two whispered to number three.
But as he turned and said *"Lord, Lord"*
God answered, *"Depart from me."*

Once again an angel appeared,
And led the second person out.
The third person in line understandably
Began to feel some doubt.

But she straightened her shoulders, remembering
All the good works she had done in the community.
Lifting her head, she looked toward the throne,
But God called her a worker of iniquity!

After the angel took her out, the fourth one in the line,
Had the urge to turn and run.
But with a shaky voice he whispered, *"Lord, Lord"*
And the Lord answered back, *"Well done."*

"My good and faithful servant,
You alone have done My will,
Knowing that some day My word
Would surely be fulfilled."

When the Lord finished speaking, the angel guarding
The door marked Eternity,
Opened it wide for the fourth person in line,
And he walked through with glee.

I hope this poetic recap of my dream
Has clearly made you see,
That all your good works, all your time spent in church,
Is not an divine guarantee.

Heaven is not like benefits
You get for working on a job.
Heaven is living in eternity
For "doing life" on earth with God.

You must daily do the Father's will
By obeying the word of God.
To enter into the kingdom of heaven
And spend eternity with Christ.

"Many will say to Me in that day, 'Lord, Lord, have we not prophesied in Your name,
cast out demons in Your name, and done many wonders in Your name?'
And then I will declare to them, 'I never knew you;
Depart from Me, you who practice lawlessness!'"

Matthew 7:22-23

UPON THIS ROCK

Matthew 7:24-29

The bible says those who hear God's word
And make the choice to obey,
Are like the wise man who built a house
Upon a rock one day.

Once he was finished, the wind began to blow,
And suddenly it was raining.
The floods began to rise as well,
But the house could not be shaken.

It didn't fall, God's word declares,
Because it was built upon a rock.
His house was safe, but down the street,
His neighbor was in for a shock.

Because his neighbor was a foolish man,
Like those who disobey.
He built his house on sand
Not caring how it was laid.

The same winds blew, the same rain came down,
And the floods were also the same.
But immediately his house fell down
And the fall of it was great.

Our lives will have the samr result
If we build on a weak foundation.
But we can strong if we build upon
On the Rock of our salvation.

If we live by this principle,
"Hear God's word and obey"
Then no matter what storms of life that come,
Rest, assured that we will be saved!

"Therefore whoever hears these sayings of Mine, and does them, I will liken him to a wise man who built his house on the rock: and the rain descended, the floods came, and the winds blew and beat on that house; and it did not fall, for it was founded on the rock. 'But everyone who hears these sayings of Mine, and does not do them, will be like a foolish man who built his house on the sand: and the rain descended, the floods came, and the winds blew and beat on that house; and it fell. And great was its fall.' And so it was, when Jesus had ended these sayings, that the people were astonished at His teaching, for He taught them as one having authority, and not as the scribes."
Matthew 7:24-29

YOU SHALL BE MADE WHOLE

Matthew 9:20-22

Like the woman with the issue of blood,
I suffered a burden that didn't belong to me.
I didn't spend money, but years of precious time.
I didn't go to doctors, but to friends and family.

And like the woman with the issue of blood,
Things didn't get better, they only got worse.
I didn't know there was a special anointing,
That would heal me of this curse.

But then one day I found myself at a women's retreat
And the speaker message ministered to me.
She spoke of the woman who touched His garment
And was healed of her plague immediately.

Then she looked over the audience and said,
"Anybody in here want to be healed?
Close your eyes reach out and touch Jesus
And you will find that this thing is real!"

I reached out my hands in the spirit,
And said *"Lord, break up my fallow ground."*
And like the woman whose fountain dried up within
Instantly, what a release I found!

When Jesus said *"You've been made whole."*
He wasn't just talking to the sinner man.
I found that His anointing will destroy the yoke
I found out and now I understand.

I can be made whole of afflictions
I can be made whole of unbelief.
I can be made whole of spiritual bondage.
I can be made whole of iniquity.

If I make up mind and I'm determined,
About any issue standing in my way;
If I reach and touch Jesus in the spirit,
I too can be made whole by faith.

And suddenly, a woman who had a flow of blood for twelve years came from behind and touched the hem of His garment. For she said to herself, 'If only I may touch His garment, I shall be made well.' But Jesus turned around, and when He saw her He said, 'Be of good cheer, daughter; your faith has made you whole.' And the woman was made well from that hour."

Matthew 9:20-22

COME UNTO ME

Matthew 11:28-30

Throughout the Old Testament we find
Examples of many times when,
The children of Israel were "yoked"
By slavery, by enemies, and by sin.

Now a yoke was a wooden beam,
That was connected by chains or poles,
To the necks or shoulders of oxen,
So they could pull a heavy load.

In Matthew, after Jesus rebuked the cities
Who had received miracles but still didn't believe,
He said, "All of you who labor and are heavy laden,
I will give you rest if you come unto Me."

"So take My yoke upon you" He said.
"Learn about me and you'll find,
That not only is My yoke easy,
But also that My burden is light."

Putting our hand to the plow in the spirit
Working for Jesus and obeying His will,
Is a much lighter and easier weight
Than a sinful life that cannot fulfill.

"Come to me, all you who are weary and burdened, and I will give you rest. Take my yoke upon you and learn from me, for I am gentle and humble in heart, and you will find rest for your souls. For my yoke is easy and my burden is light."

Matthew 11:28-30

MY CROSS

Matthew 16:24

My cross was getting heavy,
I could no longer bear,
The tests, the trials, the troubles,
And the worry beyond compare.

Daily I'd go before the throne,
Petitioning Him for relief.
Crying out to God
"Please, Lord, deliver me."

Then one day while I was praying,
For God to bless somebody else,
To relieve them of their burdens,
And to restore to them good health.

For a split second I put myself in their shoes,
And imagined that I had to carry,
The heavy load that weighed them down,
Instead of the one assigned to me.

That made me grateful for my burdens,
My tears, my pain, and my loss.
It made me praise God for my troubles,
It made me thank Him for my cross.

For if He gave it to me,
He must have faith in me,
To carry it with grace,
And to make Him proud of me.

My cross was tailor made for me,
Before the world was framed.
It's part of my assignment,
So I'll carry it in Jesus' name.

I'll do this for my Savior,
Because at Calvary,
For all my sins and my mistakes,
He bore the cross for me.

"Then Jesus said to His disciples, 'If anyone desires to come after Me, let him deny himself, and take up his cross, and follow Me'."

Matthew 16:24

TO WHOM IT MAY CONCERN

Matthew 24:40-42 | Luke 17:30, 34-36 | Galatians 5:7, 9

I want to paint a picture
Of something the Lord showed me.
This piece is rather lengthy
But I really want you to see.

Recently, I received a package in the mail,
And opened it to find,
A letter from the governor,
That really blew my mind.

"To whom it may concern" it said.
"This is your lucky day.
Our housing department's relocation plan,
Is finally headed your way.

"The state will pay for you to move
Into a brand new suburban home.
You won't have to pay a mortgage or utilities,
Like gas, water, electric, and phone.

"At the end of this month we will send
A moving truck to your front door,
To move you lock, stock, and barrel.
Now, who could ask for more?

"All you have to do to be ready
Is carefully follow the instructions below:
Pack all of your belongings and clean each room
Or else you cannot go."

The letter was signed *"Sincerely Yours"*
And dated the first of the month.
I put the letter away and said to myself
"I've got to get my packing and cleaning done!"

The next day I discovered that
I wasn't the only resident on the list.
Everyone on my block received the same letter
Not one of us was missed.

For the next few weeks, I was totally involved,
In packing and cleaning with care.
There were boxes, crates, mops, and rags
And ammonia everywhere.

From room to room I went,
Until there were no rooms left.
Every room was clean, every item was packed
And I still had two weeks to rest.

And those last two weeks was so peaceful,
I spent every day out doors.
Watching my neighbors rush to get ready,
While I relaxed on my front porch.

"She'll never make it," I said to myself.
"Just *look at those dirty window panes.*
And she's running around inside her house,
Cleaning like she's insane!"

"He might as well forget it" I said out loud.
"Because he's not even half packed,
And I just saw his wife leave the house,
And it doesn't look like she's coming back!"

I thought *"I'm glad I started right away,*
And finished with time to spare.
The end of the month is only two days away,
And that moving truck will be here."

When I woke up the following morning,
I decided to tell my house goodbye,
As I went from room to room,
Several things caught my eye.

I saw some dishes in the kitchen,
I didn't remember being there before.
And a half full trashcan
Behind one of the bedroom doors.

There were balls of dust in the hallway
So small they almost weren't there.
And when I looked out the livingroom window
The view was anything but clear.

Yes, I remembered what the letter said.
And it wasn't that I didn't care,
But streaky windows and dusty floors,
Should be within my margin of error.

And after all the packing and cleaning I'd done
I wasn't about to go back around,
Picking up this and wiping off that,
I was too tired to even bend down.

But lo and behold, when I went back outside,
Guess what I found out?
A neighbor said the moving truck had come and gone
I yelled, *"Girl, what are you talking about!"*

She said, *"They only moved two families,*
And honey they've been long gone!"
She walked away while I stood there wondering
If I had gotten something wrong.

Only two neighbors on this whole block?
It was more than I could take.
I went over all of the events in my mind
Slowly realizing my mistake.

I looked down the street at Mrs. Window Pane's house
But I could tell no one was there.
I guess she kept on cleaning
While I thought I had time to spare.

Then I looked the other way at Mr. Ex's house
Whose wife never did come back.
How did he manage to be ready for the moving truck?
I guess he continued to pack and pack.

I couldn't believe it, it just couldn't be,
I finished early, but got left behind!
Defeated, I turned to go back in my house,
And looked down on my porch to find:

Another letter from the governor.
I ripped it open and began to read,
"To whom it may concern,
We came while you were asleep.

"And we just couldn't understand why
You weren't ready when we came to move.
We found dirt and dust and clutter
In more than one of your rooms.

"Our previous letter clearly stated
'Pack and clean or you can't go.'
We had to take your name off the list
And give away your new home."

It was signed *"Sincerely Yours,*
P.S. Have a nice day."
Tears began to form in my eyes
But there was nothing I could say.

The chance of a lifetime down the drain,
Free mortgage and utilities,
A brand new home in the suburbs,
But nothing now for me.

Is the picture clear enough for you?
Well, let me point a few things out.
I want to be completely understood,
I don't want to leave any room for doubt.

The letters represent the Bible.
And the governor, well, that's God.
The brand new home is our mansion in the sky
And the moving truck is Jesus Christ.

The streaks in the mirror is the reason why
The view we have of ourselves is so dim.
The dishes, the dust, thr trashcan
Are those things we call *"little sins."*

God's word says just like a little leaven
Leavens the whole lump of dough,
Little sins will corrupt our spirits
If we don't let God's spirit to take control.

Little sins like gossiping, complaining,
And disobeying those in authority,
These little things will keep us out of heaven,
But yet we refuse to believe.

And let's be clear, sin is sin.
There is no difference to God between,
Murder, adultery, lying,
Or homosexuality.

The neighbors who I thought wouldn't make it,
Guess who they turned to be?
The saints of God who constantly pack,
And continue to keep their lives clean.

And me, well I represent the thousands who
When Jesus cracks the sky,
So sure they'll be caught up and others won't
Will be in for a big surprise.

So don't live your life like I did in this poem,
It was too late by the time I learned.
This poem isn't for anyone in particular
Only *to whom it may concern.*

"Then two men will be in the field: one will be taken and the other left.
Two women will be grinding at the mill: one will be taken and the other left.
Watch therefore, for you do not know what hour your Lord is coming.

Matthew 24:40-42

"Even so will it be in the day when the Son of Man is revealed. I tell you, in that night there will be two men in one bed: the one will be taken and the other will be left. Two women will be grinding together: the one will be taken and the other left. Two men will be in the field: the one will be taken and the other left."

Luke 17:30, 34-36

"You ran well. Who hindered you from obeying the truth?
A little leaven leavens the whole lump."

Galatians 5:7, 9

"WHY HAVE YOU BURIED MY WORK?"

Matthew 25:24-30

In the summer of 1996 I injured my back while trying to move a heavy piece of furniture. Afterwards, I was referred to a chiropractor for ongoing therapy, which caused me to miss almost an entire month from work. During that time one of my favorite pastimes was to organize my poems. I'd arrange them by topic, then date, then alphabetically. This would last for hours. When I was finished for the day, I'd put all the poems back in their folders until the next time. This ritual always brought me pleasure - until one fateful afternoon.

About three weeks later, I was sitting on my couch once again with poems spread all over the place when a voice asked, "*Why have you buried My work?*" Instantly, I remembered the parable in the Bible about the three servants who were given one, five and ten talents of money, respectively. Their master was going away and expected each servant to make a profit with the money he left them. When he returned, he found that the servants with two and five talents had doubled his money. Pleased, he rewarded them accordingly. Then he found out that the servant with one talent had buried it in the ground instead of increasing it because he was scared he would lose it. He was so displeased he called the servant wicked and lazy, took the one talent from him, gave it to the servant with ten talents, and threw the servant of his home (Matthew 25:14-30).

You can imagine how I felt. My favorite ritual had turned into a nightmare. As the story of the parable echoed in my spirit, I immediately fell on my knees asking God to forgive me for burying His work. In the weeks that followed, while fasting about another matter, I also sought direction from God regarding what I should do with all my poems.

After the fast, God led me to publish a poetry newsletter for single women. It was called THE COMPANION and it ran from November of 1996 to October of 2002. In 2003, I published a line of poetry calendars, called SEASONS. And since 2010 I've been blessed to publish seven collections of poetry, and three memoirs. As Apostle Paul said, "*Having therefore obtained help from the Lord, I continue to this day.*" (Acts 26:22)

"He also who had received the one talent came forward, saying, '
Master, I knew you to be a hard man, reaping where you did not sow,
and gathering where you scattered no seed, so I was afraid,
and I went and hid your talent in the ground. Here you have what is yours.'
But his master answered him, 'You wicked and slothful servant!
You knew that I reap where I haven't sown and gather where I scattered no seed?
Then you ought to have invested my money with the bankers,
and at my coming I should have received what was my own with interest
So take the talent from him and give it to him who has the ten talents.
For to everyone who has will more be given, and he will have an abundance.
But from the one who has not, even what he has will be taken away.
And cast the worthless servant into the outer darkness.
In that place there will be weeping and gnashing of teeth.'"

Matthew 25:24-30

EACH ONE, REACH ONE

Matthew 28:19

For every saint there is a sinner
Who must be witnessed to.
For every sinner there's a winner
To show them how to make it through.
Each one, reach one.

For every woman in the church,
There is a woman in the world,
Who thinks her beauty can only be measured by
Her face, her shape, and her curls.
Each one, reach one.

For every Brother, Deacon, and Minister,
There's a man out in the street,
Thinking he can only rely on crime,
To make his ends meet.
Each one, reach one.

For every child growing up in the church,
There is a child somewhere being abused,
Who will grow up into a teenager,
Mentally battered and confused.
Each one, reach one.

For every student in Sunday School,
There's a young person out there,
On alcohol, drugs, premarital sex,
Or considering suicide I fear.
Each one, reach one.

For every choir member and musician,
There's an entertainer making dough,
Misusing their God given talents,
And about Christ they'll never know.

For every sick believer that's healed,
Someone else is still in pain.
Without the faith to pray for sunshine,
They've settled for the rain.
Each one, reach one.

For every pew in church that's filled,
Someone has an empty nest at home.
Overcome with loneliness
Thinking they will always be alone.
Each one, reach one.

For everyone covered by the blood,
There is a demon in control,
Of someone else with no way out,
Of the chains that bind their soul.
Each one, reach one.

For every body that will be changed,
Someone else's bones will burn,
Because the commandments in the word of God,
They never lived, they never learned.
Each one, reach one.

For everyone on their way to heaven,
Someone else will meet a different end.
We've got to seek one, meet one, and teach one,
Until Jesus comes again.

"Go therefore and make disciples of all the nations, baptizing them in the name of the Father and the Son and the Holy Spirit, teaching them to observe all that I commanded you."

Matthew 28:19-20

MARK

NO ROOT, NO FRUIT

Mark 4:14-20

A sower went forth to sow his seeds,
They fell on different parts of the earth.
Like we must spread the gospel
And make sure God's word is heard.

Some seeds fell on the side of the road,
They didn't even touch the ground.
Birds and pigeons snatched them up,
As soon as they fell down.

Like those who hear the word of God
But it's not quite understood.
And before it can even be believed,
Satan distractions causes it to be lost for good.

Some seeds fell on rocky ground,
Where the dirt wasn't very deep.
As fast as the seeds sprung up they withered away,
Scorched from the sun and the heat.

Like those who hear God's word with joy
And endure for a little time.
But when faced with tests and trials of life,
They quickly change their mind.

Other seeds fell on thorny ground,
And although they tried to grow,
The thorns grew alongside the seeds,
And they slowly began to choke.

Like those who hear God's holy word,
And set out to go forth,
But then worldly desires overtake them,
And their fruit is of no worth.

Then there are the seeds that manage
To fall upon good ground.
They flourish in the sun, and rain, and air.
And grow up strong and sound.

Like those who hear the word of God,
And receive it as the truth.
By thirty, sixty, or one hundred fold,
They are able to bear good fruit.

The sower sows the word. And these are the ones by the wayside where the word is sown. When they hear, Satan comes immediately and takes away the word that was sown in their hearts. These likewise are the ones sown on stony ground who, when they hear the word, immediately receive it with gladness; and they have no root in themselves, and so endure only for a time. Afterward, when tribulation or persecution arises for the word's sake, immediately they stumble. Now these are the ones sown among thorns; they are the ones who hear the word, and the cares of this world, the deceitfulness of riches, and the desires for other things entering in choke the word, and it becomes unfruitful. But these are the ones sown on good ground, those who hear the word, accept it, and bear fruit: some thirtyfold, some sixty, and some a hundred."
Mark 4:14-20

"WHAT ABOUT THE SPICES?"

Mark 16:1-7

Sermons have different effects on us. Some inspire us to do better; some encourage us in trying times; some empower us in times of a spiritual drought. And every once in a while, we hear a sermon that makes such an impact on us that it becomes part of our every day life. *"What About The Spices?"* is one such sermon.

During the mid 1990's my pastor, District Elder Mark E. Jones, preached this during Resurrection season. He laid the foundation for the message by explaining the background on embalming practices of the time and how heavy those spices must have been that the women carried on the Sabbath following the crucifixion.

He painted a picture of the women slowing walking down the road that morning, chatting with each other about who would remove the stone from the entrance of the tomb. We could all imagine the fear and confusion as the women saw that not only had the stone already been moved, but so had the body that the spices were for (Jesus). We know from scripture that they had a heavenly encounter with an angel who told them that Jesus was not there – He had risen.

The last half of the sermon addressed the topic, *"What about the spices?"* Elder Jones talked about how we sometimes worry about something we have to do in the future—from a simple task to a great responsibility—and how we stress ourselves out only to find when the time arrives, we were worried for nothing. Sometimes because our need had already been met. Other times our contribution wasn't even required. Like the spices the women carried. As they walked, they wondered who would move the stone so they could wrap the body in spices, only to find that the stone had already been moved and the body was no longer there. The need for spices was no longer a factor. Turns out they were worried for naught.

That message is just as relevant now as it was then. More than 20 years have passed and not a week goes by that I don't find myself whispering, "What about the spices?" to stop myself from being worried or anxious about something that I have to do. And it helps every time.

"Now when the Sabbath was past, Mary Magdalene, Mary the mother of James, and Salome bought spices, that they might come and anoint Him. Very early in the morning, on the first day of the week, they came to the tomb when the sun had risen. And they said among themselves, 'Who will roll away the stone from the door of the tomb for us?' But when they looked up, they saw that the stone had been rolled away—for it was very large. And entering the tomb, they saw a young man clothed in a long white robe sitting on the right side; and they were alarmed. But he said to them, 'Do not be alarmed. You seek Jesus of Nazareth, who was crucified. He is risen! He is not here. See the place where they laid Him. But go, tell His disciples and Peter that He is going before you into Galilee; there you will see Him, as He said to you.'"

Mark 16:1-7

LUKE

MARY, MARY, QUITE CONTRARY

Luke 1:38

A girl by the name of Mary was probably,
Looking forward to her wedding day.
I'll bet she could talk of nothing else,
Since the day she got engaged.

Joseph was her fiancé,
And as a carpenter, he made a living.
I'm sure everyone in town thought he was
Loyal, faithful, and giving.

I imagine Mary couldn't wait to get married,
And fill their home with children.
She may have even planned to share them with,
Her barren cousin Elizabeth.

Perhaps Mary had it all planned.
Isn't this what every girl dreams for?
Until an angel sent by God
Walked though her living room door.

"Greetings Mary, you are highly favored!
The Lord is with you," He declared.
"Don't be afraid, you have favor with God,"
He continued, sensing her fear.

"You'll conceive and have a son;
Jesus will be his name.
He'll be given the throne of David
And forever His kingdom will reign."

Mary must've thought: *"Me and Joseph and baby boy!*
I'll be a mother and a wife!
And our son will have a throne and a kingdom?
Sounds like we will be set for life!

"But wait - the angel never mentioned Joseph -
He only mentioned me."
That's when Mary began to wonder
How it would all come to be.

"How will this all happen, Mr. Angel?
I have never been with a man."
Then with prophetic words from heaven,
The angel explained God's plan:

"The Holy Ghost shall come upon you,
And you'll be overshadowed by,
The power of the Highest,
And you will bring forth the Son of God."

Mary must have looked astonished,
Because the angel went on to say,
"With God nothing is impossible.
Elizabeth has even conceived in her old age."

Now, if you or I were in Mary's shoes,
What would have been our reply?
"No shower, no wedding, no honeymoon?
Angel, you must be out of your mind!"

But Mary, in whom God found favor;
Mary who was blessed above the rest;
Said, *"Be it unto me according to Thy will."*
And with that response she passed the test.

She willing to postpone her dreams,
She was willing to put off her plans
She was willing to face public humiliation,
And put herself completely in God's hand.

Mary didn't whine and whimper;
Mary didn't murmur and complain;
After the angel left, she went to see Elizabeth,
And glorified God with a song of praise.

One day we will be where Mary was,
About to follow through with our plans,
And God will tell us to do something
We won't quite understand.

Will we listen to the voice of God?
Will we obey His still calm voice?
Will we gladly put off something we want to do
And on top of that, rejoice?

Will our actions, like Mary's, say to God,
"Thy will be done in my life.
Lord, I put Your will before
My desire to become a husband or wife."?

Right now, you say *"Yes,"* but remember,
As you think of what you're praying for,
God wants to know that you want His will,
More than what you have asked Him for.

"Then Mary said, 'Behold the maidservant of the Lord!
Let it be to me according to your word.'"

Luke 1:38

REACH OUT
Luke 10:1-2,9

When Jesus first sent His disciples out,
He sent them out into the land,
To preach and teach the gospel, because
"The kingdom of God is at hand."

He gave them power to heal diseases.
And power to raise the dead.
He told them not to worry about money
"Freely ye have received, freely ye give."

Before Jesus departed from His disciples,
He said *"Preach the gospel to every creature."*
He also told them all of the signs
That would follow a true believer.

His last words before He ascended were,
"Lo, I am with you always."
And everything Jesus told them
Applies to us today.

We must reach out to unbelievers.
If you can't preach, then testify.
Tell of the goodness of Jesus,
Tell how He saved your life.

Reach must out to the backsliders
Tell them Jesus said, *"Come back home."*
Remind them they must be ready
Because He is soon to come.

Reach out when God leads you to a stranger.
Or when you know God sent one your way.
You may think your mind will go blank,
But God will tell you what to say.

Reach out to the sick, the shut-in,
And those having a hard time in life.
The word of God tells us to comfort others,
With the comfort we have received from Christ.

Reach out in your community.
Spread God's word there too, don't stop.
Go to one of those block meetings,
And tell them about your angelic neighborhood watch.

Reach out every chance you get,
It's not that hard to do.
And when you reach, reach out in love
Like Jesus reached out to you.

"After these things the Lord appointed seventy others also, and sent them two by two before His face into every city and place where He Himself was about to go. Then He said to them, 'The harvest truly is great, but the laborers are few; therefore pray the Lord of the harvest to send out laborers into His harvest. Heal the sick there, and say to them, "The kingdom of God has come near to you".'"

Luke10:1-2,9

COME BACK HOME

Luke 15:21-24

Do you recall the parable
Of the father and his two sons?
One demanded his inheritance early.
He wanted to take the money and run.

Soon he wasted all of his possessions,
And spent all the money he had.
The bible says, *"He began to be in want."*
Then a famine spread throughout the land.

He later went back home to his father,
Sorry for all the wrong things he did,
Realizing how unworthy he was,
And feeling guilty and sorry within.

His father hugged him and kissed him,
And ordered his servants to bring,
A robe, some shoes, and a fatted calf,
The best of everything!

He said *"This is the son I thought was dead,*
But he's come back home again.
He once was lost, but now he is found.
Let's eat and be merry, my friends!"

Perhaps you may be feeling
Just like that prodigal son;
You decided strike out on your own in this world
Thinking you didn't need anyone.

Maybe now you're tired of the way you're living,
And you're ready to renounce your life of sin;
You want to come home to the Father
Confess your sins and repent.

You have a rich Father up in heaven
Who has been waiting just for you.
To give your heart, mind, and soul to Him
And this is what He will do:

He's got a robe of righteousness to put on you,
And shoes prepared with the gospel of peace.
And his fatted calf - the word of God,
Tastes better than any meat!

If you're dead in your sins, He'll awake you.
If you're lost, you can be found again.
God will hug you and kiss you with His anointing
And bring your riotous living to an end.

"But the father said to his servants, 'Bring out the best robe and put it on him, and put a ring on his hand and sandals on his feet. And bring the fatted calf here and kill it, and let us eat and be merry; For this my son was dead and is alive again; he was lost and is found.' And they began to be merry."

Luke 15:22-24

TELL THEM
Luke 16:27-31

[Inspired by the parable of the rich man and Lazarus. Written for use in the play *"The Truth, The Whole Truth and Nothing But the Truth"* written by Felicia Lisa Middleton @ 1992; Used with permission.]

And just like that, her life was over.
I wanted to talk to her soul.
There were so many things I wanted to ask her,
So many things I wanted to know.

I asked her if she had time to pray
While the bullet traveled through the air.
Then I nodded my head in understanding
When she said *"I was totally unaware."*

I'd cried, *"Why you? Why now?*
You were young. You were just having fun."
Then I cried even harder when she whispered,
"But I didn't obey God's Son."

I asked her, *"Where are you right now?"*
"Are you resting in the bosom of Christ?"
Then I gasped as she answered,
"You know where I am, and you know why."

I asked her if she had any regrets,
Anything she would have done differently.
And I nodded my head when she admitted,
"I would have taken God's word seriously."

I listened as she tried to explain
Why she thought she could slip and slide:
"I didn't think all that stuff was important.
But I sure understand it now."

Then I asked her if there was anything
She wanted me to tell her loved ones and friends.
I shuddered as she answered,
"Tell them I never want to see them again.

"Tell them they still have time to repent,
But for me, it is too late.
Tell them I said to get right with God now,
And do not hesitate.

"Tell them to stop giving in to peer pressure,
Because the crowd can't save their souls.
Tell them don't be ashamed of the gospel of Christ,
Be proud to have the Holy Ghost.

"And tell them goodbye, because I have to go.
You know what's waiting for me."
Her voice and image faded away
And I was left crying miserably.

"Then he said, 'I beg you therefore, father, that you would send him to my father's house, for I have five brothers, that he may testify to them, lest they also come to this place of torment.' Abraham said to him, 'They have Moses and the prophets; let them hear them.' And he said, 'No, father Abraham; but if one goes to them from the dead, they will repent.' But he said to him, 'If they do not hear Moses and the prophets, neither will they be persuaded though one rise from the dead.'"

Luke 16:27-31

IN REMEMBRANCE OF ME

Luke 22:19-20

When Jesus knew His time had come,
He called His disciples together,
On the eve of the Feast of Unleavened Bread,
To have what we call The Last Supper.

As they were eating, Jesus took some bread,
Blessed it and said, *"Divide and eat.*
This is a symbol of My broken body.
Do this in remembrance of Mee."

Then Jesus took a cup of wine,
Gave thanks for it and said,
"Drink this, it's the cup of the new testament.
For many will My blood be shed."

Next, Jesus filled a basin with water,
And wrapped a towel around His waist.
He knelt and washed His disciples' feet,
As an example to be obeyed.

No matter what position we hold in life
We should see each other equally
He said, *"You'll be blessed and you'll be happy,*
If you do this in remembrance of Me."

"And He took bread, gave thanks and broke it, and gave it to them, saying,
'This is My body which is given for you; do this in remembrance of Me.'
Likewise He also took the cup after supper, saying,
'This cup is the new covenant in My blood, which is shed for you.'"

Luke 22:19-20

"Jesus rose from supper and laid aside His garments, took a towel and girded Himself. After that, He poured water into a basin and began to wash the disciples' feet, and to wipe them with the towel with which He was girded.
So when He had washed their feet, taken His garments, and sat down again, He said to them, 'Do you know what I have done to you? You call Me Teacher and Lord, and you say well, for so I am. If I then, your Lord and Teacher, have washed your feet, you also ought to wash one another's feet. For I have given you an example, that you should do as I have done to you. Most assuredly, I say to you, a servant is not greater than his master; nor is he who is sent greater than he who sent him. If you know these things, blessed are you if you do them'."

John 13:4-5;12-17

HE PRAYED FOR YOU AND ME

Luke 22:31-32 | 1 Peter 5:8-9

The voice was calm and the voice was still:
"Satan wants to devour you."
Right after that I heard a roar,
To prove that the voice was true.

Following the roar it spoke again:
"Satan wants to sift you as wheat."
I had been sitting in on the edge of my bed,
But that made me jump up on my feet.

I reached for the lamp and the Bible at the same time
And fell on my knees to pray.
Pleading the blood of Jesus against
Whatever calamity was coming my way.

After I prayed I searched my bible,
And looked up the second warning first.
It didn't take long for me to find
The book, the chapter, and the verse.

According to Luke, after last supper,
The night Jesus blessed the wine and bread,
After speaking to all the disciples,
Jesus turned to Peter and said:

"Satan desires to have you
That he may sift you as one does wheat.
But so that thy faith will not fail,
I have prayed for thee."

Jesus warned Peter that he would deny Him,
And left him with these instructions:
"After you are converted
Strengthen your brethren."

Then I looked up the first warning,
The one that was followed with a roar.
It's in Peter's first letter to the persecuted saints
Nearby and scattered abroad.

Peter warns his brethren to be sober,
Because the devil, their adversary,
Is walking to and fro like a roaring lion
Hunting for prey to eat.

Peter told the that believers everywhere
Should resist the devil by faith.
To remember they're not alone in their fight
But in God they would find grace.

He said, *"After ye have suffered awhile*
You will be perfected and established in Him."
Not only that but they would also be,
"Settled and strengthened."

The voice of the Lord that night was a reminder,
That whatever Satan attempts to do,
Our faith won't fail simply because,
He prayed for Peter, for me, and for you.

"And the Lord said, 'Simon, Simon! Indeed, Satan has asked for you, that he may sift you as wheat. But I have prayed for you, that your faith should not fail; and when you have returned to Me, strengthen your brethren.'"

Luke 22:31-32

"Be sober, be vigilant; because your adversary the devil walks about like a roaring lion, seeking whom he may devour. Resist him, steadfast in the faith, knowing that the same sufferings are experienced by your brotherhood in the world."

1 Peter 5:8-9

BEFORE THE CROSS
Luke 23:1, 7, 11, 20, 21, 24

Every Resurrection Sunday,
We remember the old rugged cross.
We celebrate the fact that for our sins,
Jesus died and paid the cost.

We sing about how He was hung up high,
And how His arms were stretched out wide.
We gratefully consider the moment when,
He gave up the ghost and died.

But as for me, I also remember the things
That happened the night before,
From the time that He was captured,
To the time He arrived at governor's palace door.

Before the cross, He was betrayed by Judas
With that famous kiss of death.
The chief priests and elders grabbed Him,
And His disciples turned and left.

Jesus was tied up and taken to the high priest
By guards with swords, and knives, and staves.
He was blindfolded, beat up, and spit on.
He was even slapped in the face.

After that they taunted Him by saying,
"Can You prophesy who slapped You?"
They mocked Him and then beat Him some more,
And they blasphemed against Him, too.

The next day they took Him to the governor,
Where it was finally decided He should die.
The governor actually found no fault in Him,
But allowed the crowd to decide.

The crowd demanded the release of a murderer
Barabbas was his name
As for Jesus – who was guilty of nothing
They cried, "*Crucify Him*" again and again.

They stripped Jesus down to almost nothing,
And beat His back with a whip.
After all of that, they nailed Him to the cross,
Then they spit on Him again.

They placed a crown of thorns upon His head,
And gave Him vinegar to drink.
All the while yelling obscenities,
With death at the very brink.

As Jesus hung there enduring all of this
The crowd didn't believe He was God's Son.
"Save yourself and come down from that cross,
If you're really God's chosen one!"

A few seconds later, He gave up the ghost.
Yet, still they weren't satisfied.
They stabbed His body with a sword
To make sure that He really died.

So each time we remember the Lamb of God
And how He paid the ultimate cost,
Let's not forget all that He endured
Before He endured the cross.

Then the whole multitude of them arose and led Him to Pilate. And as soon as he knew that He belonged to Herod's jurisdiction, he sent Him to Herod, who was also in Jerusalem at that time. Then Herod, with his men of war, treated Him with contempt and mocked Him, arrayed Him in a gorgeous robe, and sent Him back to Pilate. Pilate, therefore, wishing to release Jesus, again called out to them.
But they shouted, saying, "Crucify Him, crucify Him!"
So Pilate gave sentence that it should be as they requested.

Luke 23:1, 7, 11, 20, 21, 24

JOHN

FULL COME

John 2:4; 7:6, 8, 30, 8:20, 12:27

Throughout the gospel of St. John
Jesus says, *"My time is not yet come."*
Up until the last supper when He said,
"Father, Thy will be done."

At the marriage celebration, Mary came to Him
As He performed the first miracle of His time,
He responsed, *"My hour is not yet come."*
Before He turned the water into wine.

As the Jews sought to take his life
During the Tabernacle Feast,
Because His hour was not yet come,
He went to the temple to teach.

After Jesus met the woman at the well,
He spoke in the temple when He was done.
And no man laid hold upon Him
Because His time wasn't yet come.

Five days before the last Passover
Jesus arrived back in Jerusalem.
He said *"Shall I ask the Father to save me from this hour,*
When for this hour I have come?"

After the last supper with His disciples.
He prayed in the Garden of Gethsemane,
Saying, *"Father, if it is possible, would You*
Let this cup be passed from Me?

"Nevertheless, not My will,
But, Father, let Thy will be done."
From being betrayed to rising from the grave,
It was for this cause He had come.

"Jesus said to her, 'Woman, what does your concern have to do with Me? My hour has not yet come.'"

John 2:4

"Then Jesus said to them, 'My time has not yet come, but your time is always ready.'"

John 7:6

"You go up to this feast. I am not yet going up to this feast, for My time has not yet fully come."

John 7:8

"Therefore they sought to take Him; but no one laid a hand on Him, because His hour had not yet come."

John 7:30

"These words Jesus spoke in the treasury, as He taught in the temple; and no one laid hands on Him, for His hour had not yet come."

John 8:20

"Now My soul is troubled, and what shall I say? 'Father, save Me from this hour'? But for this purpose I came to this hour.'"

John 12:27

THE OVERFLOW

John 7:37-39

I'm as dry as the dirt in the desert,
I'm dying of thirst from within,
For too long I've quenched the anointing,
It's not even really about sin.
I'm in need of an overflow.

I'm too tired of going through the motions,
And playing my part so well,
That I've almost fooled myself,
Even though others can't seem to tell,
I'm in need of an overflow.

Too stubborn to admit any weakness,
Too proud to let anyone know,
Too ashamed to admit after all this time,
I'm in need of an overflow.

But, has it been so long that I've forgotten,
Any time I am in need,
You are willing and able and ready,
My emptiness to receive?

And have my eyes become so blinded,
And has my memory become so foggy,
That I forgot You said in Your word,
You'd be a well of water inside of me?

How much longer will it be until I seek You,
Surrender my will and control,
Lay down the weights and the sin that's beset me,
And receive an overflow?

Even now I can feel Your conviction,
Gently pulling and tugging my soul,
And I know that Your loving chastisement,
Will be followed by an overflow.

(And it was.)

"On the last day, that great day of the feast, Jesus stood and cried out, saying,
'If anyone thirsts, let him come to Me and drink. He who believes in Me, as the
Scripture has said, out of his heart will flow rivers of living water.'
But this He spoke concerning the Spirit, whom those believing in Him would receive;
for the Holy Spirit was not yet given, because Jesus was not yet glorified."

John 7:37-39

THE OPEN DOOR POLICY

John 10:7-9

Recently I transferred to a new office,
When I noticed an interesting thing,
A sign on the manager's door that said
"An open door policy."

This boss said we should always,
Feel free to walk right in,
He said no matter what he's doing,
He'd greet us with a smile and a grin.

"An open door policy" I said aloud,
And taking a deep breath, I walked in.
And although he was on the phone,
He looked up, gave a wave and a grin.

My boss doesn't know it but he's a lot like Christ,
Who also has an open door policy.
Like an open door, His arms stretched wide
When He hung on Calvary.

Jesus is the open door to salvation,
Today His arms are still stretched out wide,
Saying *"Come unto me ye that are heavy laden,*
And beneath My wings abide."

Jesus has more than just one open door,
There are many open doors for me and you.
Every scripture is an open door,
To His divine promises and blessings.

"God will supply all your need"
That's a door stretched open wide.
But many of us still stand in need because
We lack the faith that He will provide.

If you have a financial need,
There's an open door just for you.
Not only a door, but the windows of heaven.
(I know it sounds unbelievable, but it's true.)

There's an open door with a sign that says:
"By his stripes we were healed."
And we can walk through with confidence
No matter how sick we may feel.

Yes, every scripture is an open door,
Where we can all feel free,
To walk by faith believing
That what we ask, we will receive.

"Then Jesus said to them again, 'Most assuredly, I say to you, I am the door of the sheep. All who ever came before Me are thieves and robbers, but the sheep did not hear them. I am the door. If anyone enters by Me, he will be saved, and will go in and out and find pasture.'"

John 10:7-9

LIFT JESUS UP
John 12:32

Sometimes we tend to worry,
About bringing lost souls in.
When Jesus said if He be lifted up,
He'd draw all men to Him.

In context what Jesus really meant
Is that His death upon the cross
Would be the catalyst of the salvation
And the redemption of the lost.

They should not be angrily greeted with
"You must be born again!"
They should never be threatened with
"You're going to hell if you continue in sin!"

And I know we're Apostolic
But that's not where we should begin.
Just focus on how much Jesus loves them
That He suffered, bled and died for them.

Tell how your soul hungered for something,
Until He invited you to sit and sup.
Tell how your life was empty,
Until He overflowed your cup.

If we concentrate on lifting Jesus up,
And telling of the good things He's done,
If we plant the seed of interest,
Testify and move on;

Then we'll be sure to spark some interest,
Folks will want to meet Jesus too.
And I'm sure they'll want the Holy ghost,
After hearing how God saved you.

"And I, if I am lifted up from the earth, will draw all peoples to Myself."
John 12:32

SHOW GOD'S LOVE

John 13:35

As I look around the body of Christ,
It grieves my heart to see,
Attitudes, disputes, and grudges,
Between saints that God set free.

The first fruit of the Spirit,
The first proof that Christ lives within,
Is the love that we have for God
And for our brethren.

Seventy times seventy is the principle
Of how we should forgive one another.
But how can we expect God to forgive us
When we won't forgive each other?

How can we sit in any service,
And truly praise the Lord,
When we still have unsettled disputes
And we're not on one accord?

But if we learn to hold our peace,
And keep our minds on Him,
God will work out our differences ,
And give us peace without and within.

I say this because I have been there,
But then God let me know,
That if I pray and ask Him,
He will cause my love to grow.

He will melt everything in me,
That shouldn't really be there.
He'll replace it with His love,
He'll replace it with His care.

Believe it or not, I have to do this
Almost each and every day.
This is what it means to die daily
And let God direct the way.

Each time I start to say something,
Negative about someone else,
I stop - sometimes in mid-sentence -
And silently ask the Lord for help.

God's love can melt our anger
It can settle every dispute,
It can forever bury every grudge
And every nasty attitude.

Because the moment that Jesus cracks the sky
None of us want to be
Left behind because of vengeful, hateful heart
That could have been redeemed.

"By this all will know that you are My disciples, if you have love for one another."
John 13:35

JESUS IS THE ANSWER

John 14:6

Many questions go unanswered
In this world in which we live.
But Jesus Christ is really
The only answer we can give.

He's the answer to the question,
"Who will care for those living on the street?"
For He alone can save and bless them
With the new life and home they all need.

He's the answer to the question,
"What about those strung out on crack?"
He alone has the power to deliver them
And to get their lives back on track.

He's the answer to the question,
"Do we need gun control?"
Not only can He protect us better,
He can also save every gun carrier's soul.

He's the answer to the question,
"What do we do about teen pregnancy?"
There is hope for unwed parents
Because His blood alone redeems.

He's the answer to the question,
"Will I ever get out of debt?"
If we're faithful in our giving He will bless us
In ways we will never forget.

Yes, many questions go unanswered
This is true indeed
But only because people don't realize
That Jesus is exactly what they need.

"Jesus said to him, 'I am the way, the truth, and the life.
No one comes to the Father except through Me.'"

John 14:6

THE COMFORTER HAS COME

John 14:16, 26; 15:26; 16:7-8

Before Jesus was betrayed
He said a Comforter would come,
Sent by God the Father,
Sent in the name of the Son.

He told all of His disciples
That He had to go away.
He said if He did not go then He could not send
This Comforter their way.

Jesus said *"I will not leave you comfortless,*
I will return unto you.
I will abide with you forever,
And dwell within you too."

He said that this Comforter
Would testify of Him,
That it would be called the Spirit of Truth,
And would reprove the world of sin.

Well, Jesus is that Comforter,
He guides us into all truth,
He delivers us from all evil,
And our sin He does rebuke.

Jesus is that Comforter,
He shows us things to come,
He testifies of Himself through us,
Each time we speak in tongues.

God manifested Himself to flesh,
And that flesh died for our sins,
Then that flesh rose and became the Comforter,
So He would always dwell within.

"And I will pray the Father, and he shall give you another Comforter, that he may abide with you forever."

John 14:16 KJV

"But the Comforter, which is the Holy Ghost, whom the Father will send in my name, he shall teach you all things, and bring all things to your remembrance, whatsoever I have said unto you."

John 14:26 KJV

"But when the Comforter is come, whom I will send unto you from the Father, even the Spirit of truth, which proceedeth from the Father, he shall testify of me."

John 15:26 KJV

"Nevertheless I tell you the truth; It is expedient for you that I go away: for if I go not away, the Comforter will not come unto you; but if I depart, I will send him unto you. And when he is come, he will reprove the world of sin, and of righteousness, and of judgment:"

John 16:7-8 KJV

THE TRUE VINE
John 15:1

Jesus is the True Vine,
And God is the Husbandman.
We are the branches that grow from
The root of the vine, God's Son.

Like a branch that bears no fruit,
Is destined to wither away,
Those of us who don't abide on the vine
Won't have the strength to stay.

But those us who do bear fruit,
And find the strength to stay,
God will purge us and renew us,
And allow us to remain.

Without Him we can do nothing,
But if we remain connected to the root,
And endeavor to abide in the vine,
He will help us bear good fruit.

I am the true vine, and my Father is the husbandman.
John 15:1

I HAVE A FRIEND

John 15:13-15

I have a friend who's always near,
Whenever I'm in need.
I can call Him up, knowing that
He will be there for me.

I have a friend who never changes,
Except to get sweeter every day.
I know that if I ever get lost,
He'll point me the right way.

I have a friend who I can trust,
I can tell Him anything.
He's my number one confidant,
With each and everything.

I have a friend who's honest,
He tells me when I'm wrong.
He chastises me and corrects me,
And loves me all along.

I have a friend I can count on,
No matter what I'm going through.
I can go to Him for advice,
He always tells me the right thing to do.

I have a friend above all others,
He laid down His life for me.
My friend's name is Jesus Christ,
The man from Galilee.

"Greater love has no one than this, than to lay down one's life for his friends. You are My friends if you do whatever I command you. No longer do I call you servants, for a servant does not know what his master is doing; but I have called you friends, for all things that I heard from My Father I have made known to you."

John 15:13-15

ACTS

A LIVING WITNESS

Acts 1:8

People all across this world
Have wants and needs inside.
We must tell them that we found joy
Now that in Christ we abide.

We can be a living witness ,
For those who are in need,
By the way we live before them,
By the things in us they see.

We should be hungry for the Holy Ghost,
And hungry to do God's will,
Thirsty for a fresh anointing,
Starving every day to be filled.

Our souls should long for the living God,
Our hearts should beat only for Him,
If we daily yield to His spirit,
We'll have the strength not to yield to sin.

There should always be a need within us
To call His name out loud in prayer,
Our lips should always be ready to praise Him
Any place, anytime, anywhere.

For then and only then,
Will this world really see,
That Jesus Christ is the answer,
To everything they need.

"But ye shall receive power, after that the Holy Ghost is come upon you: and ye shall be witnesses unto me both in Jerusalem, and in all Judaea, and in Samaria, and unto the uttermost part of the earth."

Acts 1:8

A PERSONAL PENTECOST

Acts 2:1-4

After Jesus died and rose,
He showed Himself for forty days,
Saying, "*Teach my gospel to every nation*
But first in Jerusalem you must wait."

"*Wait for the promise of My Father.*
Wait for My power from on high.
Wait for John's prophesy to be fulfilled.
Wait for the baptism of the Holy Ghost and fire."

Then Jesus was caught up into heaven,
After He had spoken all of these words.
And the disciples and over 100 others,
Continued in prayer on one accord.

And exactly ten days later,
The day of Pentecost had arrived.
Wind from heaven filled the room
And they saw flaming tongues of fire.

The tongues separated and sat on each of them,
And they were filled with the Holy ghost.
They began to speak divinely in other languages,
And of God's wonderful works did they boast.

Peter let the doubters know they were not drunk,
It was just past scriptures coming true,
Of God pouring out His spirit upon all flesh,
Just like He's done for me and you.

At one time or another many of us have had
A personal Pentecost,
When God touched us with tongues of fire,
And were no longer lost.

We had a day that was like no other,
When God's Spirit took control.
We discovered that other Comforter,
And now we want the world know:

That if you believe that Jesus Christ
Died to save you from your sins,
Today you can meet the Comforter,
And welcome Him to come within.

If you're reading this and you know
That your life is in need of a change,
Today can be your very own
Pentecostal day.

"When the Day of Pentecost had fully come, they were all with one accord in one place. And suddenly there came a sound from heaven as of a rushing mighty wind, and it filled the whole house where they were sitting. Then there appeared to them divided tongues, as of fire, and one sat upon each of them. And they were all filled with the Holy Spirit and began to speak with other tongues, as the Spirit gave them utterance."

Acts 2:1-4

TRUE LOVE PENTECOST

Acts 2:5-8, 11-18, 21

We came from several different states,
But our intentions were the same,
We had gathered together that weekend,
To fellowship in Jesus' name.

Our presiding Apostle preached two nights in a row,
And the spirit was really high.
By the time the weekend was over,
We all knew the reason why.

It started with one soul getting saved,
Saturday night after the altar call.
I could see the joy all over her face,
As her tears continued to fall.

By Sunday night excitement was in the air,
And with each spiritual station break,
We were all kept updated as,
Even more souls were saved.

Elders shouted in the pulpit,
Mother's cried out from the floor,
And I didn't think it was possible,
But God poured out His Spirit some more.

During offering time as I went around,
I took my daughter by the hand,
And said "Let's run to the ladies room now,
So we won't miss anything, understand?"

As I opened the door of the ballroom,
I could see just past the entrance,
A crowd of young people speaking in tongues,
As God's Spirit gave the utterance.

I went to hug a sister,
And the Spirit touched me too.
Jesus started speaking through me,
And I was refilled anew.

We all hugged each other,
More times than we realized,
Yet still the Spirit continued to move,
As more tears fell from our eyes.

A few hotel guests squeezed past us,
And hotel employees passed on by.
I wondered if they thought that we,
Were drunk with new wine.

Needless to say, things settled down,
And back into service we went,
And the message that night, *"Restore Your Joy"*
Was surely heaven sent.

God had poured out His Spirit upon all flesh,
Not just on the souls newly saved,
But also on those of us already filled,
He restored our joy and our praise.

We witnessed the true love of Jesus.
We witnessed the saving of souls that were lost.
We witnessed Him quicken our very own spirits.
We witnessed a True Love Pentecost!

"And there were dwelling in Jerusalem Jews, devout men, from every nation under heaven. And when this sound occurred, the multitude came together, and were confused, because everyone heard them speak in his own language. Then they were all amazed and marveled, saying to one another, 'Look, are not all these who speak Galileans? And how is it that we hear, each in our own language in which we were born? We hear them speaking in our own tongues the wonderful works of God.' So they were all amazed and perplexed, saying to one another, 'Whatever could this mean?' Others mocking said, 'They are full of new wine.'"

"But Peter, standing up with the eleven, raised his voice and said to them, 'Men of Judea and all who dwell in Jerusalem, let this be known to you, and heed my words. For these are not drunk, as you suppose, since it is only the third hour of the day. But this is what was spoken by the prophet Joel: "And it shall come to pass in the last days, says God, That I will pour out of My Spirit on all flesh; Your sons and your daughters shall prophesy, Your young men shall see visions, Your old men shall dream dreams. And on My menservants and on My maidservants I will pour out My Spirit in those days; And they shall prophesy. And it shall come to pass That whoever calls on the name of the Lord shall be saved".'"

Acts 2:5-8; 11-18; 21

(In honor of the Lift Him Up True Love Fellowship, New Brunswick, N.J., and hosts Bishops Bradfor Berry and Bishop Fred Rubin)

THE SPIRIT OF UNITY

Acts 2:44-47; 4:31-32

On the day of Pentecost when the Holy ghost fell,
They were all in one place on one accord,
And they were all baptized by God's Spirit,
Into the body of Jesus Christ our Lord.

A few days later, after Peter & John were released,
From behind the local prison walls.
With one accord they prayed unto God,
And once again, God's Spirit filled them all.

God's word says that the multitude of believers,
Were of one heart, one mind and one soul.
And whether in the temple or house to house,
They continued daily on one accord.

Today we can have that same kind of unity,
That same kind of fellowship in the church.
We can have God's power poured upon us,
If we do what they did, it will work.

Unity like that can only begin,
When we unite ourselves in Christ.
When individually we are one with God's spirit,
And He alone reigns over our life.

With lowliness, meekness and longsuffering,
Forbearing one another in love,
Praying together in the spirit,
And singing praises to God above.

Then we can move as one body,
Then we can fellowship on one accord,
Then we can work together in God's kingdom,
Accomplishing the vision and the will of the Lord.

"Now all who believed were together, and had all things in common, and sold their possessions and goods, and divided them among all, as anyone had need. So continuing daily with one accord in the temple, and breaking bread from house to house, they ate their food with gladness and simplicity of heart, praising God and having favor with all the people."

Acts 2:44-47

"And when they had prayed, the place where they were assembled together was shaken; and they were all filled with the Holy Spirit, and they spoke the word of God with boldness.And the multitude of them that believed were of one heart and of one soul: neither said any of them that ought of the things which he possessed was his own; but they had all things common."

Acts 4:31-32

GOD'S HOSPITAL

Acts 3:1-10

The house of God is like a hospital,
Where sin sick souls are healed,
Where the broken hearted find out that,
The love of God is real.

It's a place where the doctors and nurses,
Are working to do God's will,
Where whatever prescriptions are written,
They are happy just to fill.

What's different about this hospital staff,
Is that it's made up of people who,
Were once part of this sin-sick world,
But Jesus healed them too.

And after their deliverance,
Instead of going on their merry way,
They stuck around and lent a hand,
To help someone else get saved.

You'll find all types of patients there,
Admitted ones waiting to be released.
Out patients who return regularly,
Because their healing is not complete.

Those with the sickness of fornication,
Meet others who once had the same disease,
But now they testify that Jesus satisfies,
And if you want to be kept, He'll keep.

Those whose lying lips and gossiping tongues,
Kept them on a spiritual death bed,
Meet recovering ones whose tongues God tamed,
And now they speak life instead.

Every once in a while a patient is rushed,
Into the emergency room on a "Code Blue"
Because demons have taken over some poor soul,
But Jesus can heal that too.

Needles are pre-filled carefully,
With just the right dose,
Of a drug only the Chief of Staff can administer,
The gift of the Holy Ghost.

In the waiting room of this hospital,
Workers give out encouraging words,
To those who are down and out,
And to others who just want to be heard.

A few scripts are marked hugs and kisses
They're reserved for the rough and tough times
When the staff have to remind each other
That things will work out just fine.

Yes, God's house is like a hospital,
Where we all work for Him,
In a special field of medicine called
Deliverance from sin.

"Now Peter and John went up together to the temple at the hour of prayer, the ninth hour. And a certain man lame from his mother's womb was carried, whom they laid daily at the gate of the temple which is called Beautiful, to ask alms from those who entered the temple; who, seeing Peter and John about to go into the temple, asked for alms. And fixing his eyes on him, with John, Peter said, 'Look at us.' So he gave them his attention, expecting to receive something from them. Then Peter said, 'Silver and gold I do not have, but what I do have I give you: In the name of Jesus Christ of Nazareth, rise up and walk.' And he took him by the right hand and lifted him up, and immediately his feet and ankle bones received strength. So he, leaping up, stood and walked and entered the temple with them—walking, leaping, and praising God. And all the people saw him walking and praising God. Then they knew that it was he who sat begging alms at the Beautiful Gate of the temple; and they were filled with wonder and amazement at what had happened to him."

Acts 3:1-10

ABIDE IN THE SHIP

Acts 27:31

On a ship set sail for Italy ,
The one and only Apostle Paul,
Faced a mighty tempest storm at sea
And learned a lesson for us all.

Contrary winds turned dangerous,
And Paul urged them back to shore.
But no one bothered to believe him
So he withdrew—probably below.

For many days there was no sun, no stars,
The crew gave up all hope of being saved.
Then Paul returned and told them,
"You should have listened to me the other day.

"But fear not, God sent His angel
Who said not one of us will be lost.
God said I'll get to my destination
No matter what the cost."

So they continued on until they thought
They saw land straight ahead.
Then quickly threw their anchors over when,
They saw dangerous rocks instead.

The shipmen let down a life boat
And tried to sneak away.
But Paul ominously warned them
"Abide in the ship or you won't be saved."

They went on a fast and when ended it
They gave thanks and then they ate.
Afterward, they threw extra baggage overboard
To lighten the ship for the rest of the way.

Violent waves smashed against the ship
Practically breaking it all apart,
But on boards and broken pieces
Every soul made it safely to port.

Today the ship represents our lives in Christ,
And the storms are our tests along the way.
Things in our lives may be falling apart
But if we abide in the ship we will be saved.

Let's not be guilty of treason,
Cheating on God and going our own way,
Or following others who "Go overboard."
We must abide in the ship to be saved.

Don't give up and throw your anchor over.
Don't backslide and steer too far away.
Don't jump in a lifeboat to take the easy way out.
You must abide in the ship to be saved.

When life's dangerous winds blow against you,
When you're drenched in violent waves,
God may bring you to shore on broken pieces,
But if you abide in His ship you'll be saved.

"Paul said to the centurion and the soldiers,
'Unless these men stay in the ship, you cannot be saved.'"

Acts 27:31

ROMANS

PEACE IN THE STREETS

Romans 3:10-18

In these perilous times that we live in
Some people are in search of peace.
But worldly places and earthly things
Are all they constantly seem to seek.

I know there's no real peace
In the awful world of sin.
There is no remedy that will bring happiness
Or calm one's fears within.

I know because I once was
Trapped in the excitement of the streets.
Taking my fill of worldly pleasures
Thinking I had life beat.

I lived just for the weekend,
And I partied from week to week,
From man to man I looked for love
Until I made a startling discovery.

I discovered that the only cure for street life,
The only place that one should go,
Is to the foot of the cross where Jesus Christ
Can wash us white as snow.

I became addicted to Holy ghost,
And attracted to His blood,
I fell in love with His holy word
And found out what peace is made of.

Now I witness to those still caught up
In all that inner city strife
I am living proof that Christ alone
Is the only cure for street life.

"As it is written: 'There is none righteous, no, not one; There is none who understands;
There is none who seeks after God. They have all turned aside;
They have together become unprofitable; There is none who does good, no, not one.
Their throat is an open tomb; With their tongues they have practiced deceit;
The poison of asps is under their lips; Whose mouth is full of cursing and bitterness.
Their feet are swift to shed blood; Destruction and misery are in their ways;
And the way of peace they have not known. There is no fear of God before their eyes.'"

Romans 3:10-18

"DON'T CLOSE YOUR EYES"
Romans 5:8; 13:11-14

I remember the time someone put a "mickey" in my drink. I was out partying with my girls at a club, but left my drink unattended to hit the dance floor. It was the 80's, and I was young but I knew better. When I returned to my seat at the bar, there he was smiling at me like he had been waiting for me his whole life. I sat down, resumed drinking my Southern Comfort and orange juice, and smiled back at dark and handsome stranger. After some chit-chat, he asked me to dance.

When I stood up, I feel woozy. He tried to help me walk back to my seat, but somehow one of my girlfriends appeared and asked me if I was okay, did I want to go to the ladies' room. I said "No" and went outside instead. The smiling stranger followed close behind. By this time sweat was pouring from me like I had been caught in a rainstorm. The cool night air didn't help, so I stumbled back inside and made my way to the bathroom. All I wanted to do was to sit down somewhere and go to sleep.

Right there in that bathroom, a voice out of nowhere said, *"Don't close your eyes."* But I couldn't help it. I was really out of it. I closed my eyes. Then the voice said, "*Don't go to sleep*." When I heard those words, I opened my eyes to see who was there. I stood up and peeked outside the stall. No one was there. I made my way back outside, thinking the guy would be there but instead, my girlsfriends were waiting for me. One of them drove me home in my car and the other followed.

Even in my sin, when I didn't have Him on my mind, God protected me from *"Dangers seen and unseen."* Anything could have happened to me that night. Anything.

The warning not to close my eyes and not to goo to sleep was twofold. In time, I woke up ***spiritually***. In time, I opened my eyes, ***spiritually***. In time, I returned to God as the prodigal daughter that I was. And, as the lyrics to that old gospel song by Reverend James Moore says, *"He was there all the time, waiting patiently in line. The Lord was there, Jesus was there, all the time."*

*"But God demonstrates His own love toward us,
in that while we were still sinners, Christ died for us."*

Romans 5:8

"And that, knowing the time, that now it is high time to awake out of sleep: for now, is our salvation nearer than when we believed. The night is far spent, the day is at hand: let us therefore cast off the works of darkness and let us put on the armor of light. Let us walk honestly, as in the day, not in rioting and drunkenness, not in chambering and wantonness, not in strife and envying. But put ye on the Lord Jesus Christ, and make not provision for the flesh, to fulfil the lusts thereof."

Romans 13.11-14

RENEW YOUR MIND

Romans 12:2

It was a beautiful Spring day, and I was driving through my neighborhood taking it all in. Actually, I was multi-tasking while driving. No, I wasn't on the phone, or texting, or putting on make-up, or eating. I was praying. And it was one of those desperate, stomach clenching, gut wrenching "Lord-I-need-an-answer-right-now" type of prayers.

There was a desire on my heart and a decision I had to make, and I couldn't decide what to do. I remember crying "Lord, how do I know what Your will is in this situation? How do I know Lord? How?"

For a while, all I heard was the traffic, the sounds of the outdoors and the sniffling of my nose.

And then the voice that I know so well spoke to me and said, "Be transformed by the renewing of your mind and you will discover My will."

Immediately, I blew my nose, wiped my tears, and made my way home, smiling all the way. God had answered and I knew what He meant: If I got more into the word, more into prayer, and more into Him, my mind would be renewed and the answer would come.

So I did, and it did.

"Do not be conformed to this world, but be transformed by the renewing of your mind, that you may prove what is that good and acceptable and perfect will of God."

Romans 12:12

IT'S ALMOST MIDNIGHT

Romans 13:11-14 | Ephesians 5:15-21 | Hebrews 3:12-15

It's 11:00 pm on the clock of your life,
And you think you've got enough time,
To do all the things you desire,
Before your life strikes midnight.

At 11:10 pm you hear the word of God,
And feel convicted deep inside,
But you fail to surrender to Jesus,
Because you think you've got enough time.

Around 11:25 pm someone you know gets saved
And tells you about God's love
But still you don't surrender
Still you don't give up.

At 11:40 pm trouble comes your way
But rather than let God in
You think things have got to get better
So you continue to live in sin.

When Jesus calls you again at 11:55 pm
You say, *"I've got five good minutes left,*
Then I'll get myself together
Then I'll definitely repent."

But in the middle of that last sentence
Your clock suddenly strikes midnight!
Too late to decide to surrender
Too late to do what's right.

All along you thought you knew
Exactly what time it was in your life,
But only God really knows
How close you are to midnight.

Midnight for some will be a time to rejoice
Because we'll spend eternity with Christ
Since we gave our lives on earth to Him
He'll give us everlasting life.

But unfortuneatly for others, midnight will be
The beginning of the end
Because after you heard the word of God
You continued to live in sin.

You think you've got twenty minutes left
Or ten or five or two,
But the very next breath that you take
Might be the last for you.

Jesus said the day you hear his voice
Harden not your heart
His voice comes through the bible,
Sermons, songs, and testimonies we impart.

So whether we're waiting for the New Year
Or for Jesus to crack the sky,
This poem is friendly reminder
To be ready for midnight.

"And do this, knowing the time, that now it is high time to awake out of sleep; for now our salvation is nearer than when we first believed. The night is far spent, the day is at hand. Therefore, let us cast off the works of darkness, and let us put on the armor of light. Let us walk properly, as in the day, not in revelry and drunkenness, not in lewdness and lust, not in strife and envy. But put on the Lord Jesus Christ, and make no provision for the flesh, to fulfill its lusts."

Romans 13:11-14

"See then that you walk circumspectly, not as fools but as wise, redeeming the time, because the days are evil. Therefore, do not be unwise, but understand what the will of the Lord is. And do not be drunk with wine, in which is dissipation; but be filled with the Spirit, speaking to one another in psalms and hymns and spiritual songs, singing and making melody in your heart to the Lord, giving thanks always for all things to God the Father in the name of our Lord Jesus Christ, submitting to one another in the fear of God."

Ephesians 5:15-21

"Therefore, as the Holy Spirit says: 'Today, if you will hear His voice do not harden your hearts as in the rebellion, In the day of trial in the wilderness, Where your fathers tested Me, tried Me, And saw My works forty years.

Beware, brethren, lest there be in any of you an evil heart of unbelief in departing from the living God; but exhort one another daily, while it is called 'Today,' lest any of you be hardened through the deceitfulness of sin. For we have become partakers of Christ if we hold the beginning of our confidence steadfast to the end, while it is said: 'Today, if you will hear His voice, Do not harden your hearts as in the rebellion.'"

Hebrews 3:12-15

DIVIDE AND CONQUER

Romans 15:17-20

Satan has launched a serious attack
Against the body of Jesus Christ.
His goal is to seek and destroy
Those who are saved and sanctified.

I see a trend that tells me,
He's moved from individual attacks,
Into pitting one against the other,
While he himself steps back.

Whenever there is division and confusion
Satan is in the midst.
We must learn to recognize his schemes
Instead of falling for his tricks.

A small misunderstanding is blown up
Into unnecessary dispute.
A few people tell a few others
And suddenly everyone is spreading the news.

We get so wrapped up in the cause
Of who is wrong and who is right.
We can't even see that Satan is attacking,
We're so busy causing strife.

Be not ignorant of Satan's devices!
Not all of us will fall,
By drugs, fornication, murder, or theft
For some of us it will be something small.

Small things like grudges we won't let go of,
Or secret sins still not confessed,
Spreading gossip, sowing seeds of discord,
And causing division among brethren.

Just like in a natural war Satan's job
Is to utterly destroy the saints.
And we play right into his hand
When we constantly fall for his games.

His master plan is to divide and conquer,
Why can't you see that you're being used?
When you go around sowing seeds of discord
But insist that everyone else is confused.

And if everybody is murmuring ,
And if everybody has a complaint,
I wonder who is praying for lost souls
To make it into the pearly gates?

If everyone has a problem with everyone else
What will lost souls see
When they comes into the house of God?
They'll hear you talking negatively about me.

They'll see one person rolling their eyes at another,
While smiling a phony *"Praise the Lord"* to them.
They'll think *"This church ain't for me,"*
And go out and continue in sin.

If you take a moment to think about it
I'm sure that you'll agree.
The fight is between us and Satan
Not between you and me.

"Now I urge you, brethren, note those who cause divisions and offenses,
contrary to the doctrine which you learned, and avoid them.
For those who are such do not serve our Lord Jesus Christ, but their own belly,
and by smooth words and flattering speech deceive the hearts of the simple.
For your obedience has become known to all. Therefore I am glad on your behalf;
but I want you to be wise in what is good, and simple concerning evil.
And the God of peace will crush Satan under your feet shortly."

Romans 16:17-20

1 Corinthians

FOOLISH THINGS

1 Corinthians 1:27-29

God takes pleasure in foolish things
Things that we think are weak.
He uses them to confuse the minds
Of the wise and the mighty.

And the lowly people of this world,
The ones who are despised,
God choses to redeem them,
And them He justifies.

Sometimes we stop and ask ourselves
"Why did God save me?
"Out of all the sinners in the world
"I must have been the chief!"

We wonder what made God decide
To give us His work to do.
Surely there was someone else more qualified
Than the likes of me or you.

Well, the almighty God that we serve,
He just loves to find,
A sinner on their way to hell,
And save them just in time.

God welcomes the broken hearted
To bring all of their pieces to Him.
For He alone has the power
To put them back together again.

God is delighted to meet the destitute,
It's a chance for Him to show,
That if we would only send the praises up
The blessings would overflow.

God gets a thrill when He can fill,
That empty void inside,
With His precious love, his unspeakable joy,
And His blessed peace of mind.

God seeks out those who are so depressed
They're on the verge of suicide,
And tells them they can have eternal life
Because Jesus already died.

God takes pleasure in discovering
People that He can clean.
He'll call a drug dealer to preach His word
He'll make a prostitute His queen.

God is happy to rescue kidnapped souls
From the very depths of hell.
Redeem their soul, renew their mind
And give them a testimony to tell.

And after God has taken all these lives,
And turned each one around,
After has taken all these feet,
And placed them on solid ground;

All God wants in return
From them, from me, from you,
Is to give Him all the honor, all the glory,
And all the praise that He is due.

For He alone is worthy
All power is in His hands.
His thoughts are not like our thoughts
His ways we can't understand.

We should remember these things the next time we think
"What did God save me for?"
So that none of us will glory in ourselves
Instead, we will glory in the Lord.

For who else but God almighty
Knew exactly which one of us,
Underneath the muck and mire of this foolish world,
Was a diamond in the rough?

"But God has chosen the foolish things of the world to put to shame the wise, and God has chosen the weak things of the world to put to shame the things which are mighty; and the base things of the world and the things which are despised God has chosen, and the things which are not, to bring to nothing the things that are, that no flesh should glory in His presence."

1 Corinthians 1:27-29

LABORING IN GOD'S KINGDOM

1 Corinthians 3:9

We work so hard in the house of God
From the pulpit to the door.
But have we ever stopped to consider,
Just what are we working for?

We overwork our bodies ,
We spend all of our time,
We use and abuse our talents,
We even give our very last last dime.

Why do we labor so endlessly
In the house and the kingdom of God?
Why do we put His work before
Our family, our friends, our jobs?

Are we working for titles, positions,
Or recognition through the land?
No, we're working for something much higher
Than simply being noticed by man.

We are working for our Master,
And our Savior Jesus Christ.
We're working for the CEO
Who reigns and rules over our lives.

We're working because the harvest is plentiful
But laborers like us are few.
And we realize God saved us because
He has someting special He wants us to do.

Something before going to glory;
Something more than just being blessed;
Something in addition to speaking in tongues;
Something besides going through trials and tests.

God has a unique work for each of us
That will reach lost, dying souls.
And in our own unique way tell them
That Jesus can make them whole.

So we labor in God's kingdom
Some of us are over worked and under paid.
Some of us work until we are burned out,
But we know our labor is not in vain.

For there's special feeling that comes over you,
When you know you're doing God's will.
And there's an anointing that God gives you
So that His will can be fulfilled.

And there's victory in serving Jesus.
Victory in earnestly doing His work.
Victory in setting aside our own agendas,
And seeking God's kingdom first.

Victory in doing our reasonable service,
Victory in doing God's will God's way,
Victory in pleasing God on earth,
And in the crown we'll get some day.

"For we are laborers together with God: ye are God's husbandry, ye are God's building."
1 Corinthians 3:9 KJV

"I have labored and toiled and have often gone without sleep; I have known hunger and thirst and have often gone without food; I have been cold and naked. Besides everything else, I face daily the pressure of my concern for all the churches."
2 Corinthians 11:27-28 NIV

SUCH WERE SOME OF YOU

1 Corinthians 6:9-11

Sometimes we use our spiritual eyes
As a window to see who,
Among other believers
Are struggling to make it through.

With judgment we shake our heads
And wonder why they are not,
Where we think they should be
In their walk with Jesus Christ.

When listen to their prayer requests
And instead of lifting up their names,
In supplication unto God
We look at them in shame.

With our mouths we condemn them,
No matter the circumstance.
We roll our eyes in judgment
Refusing to give them a second chance.

We just can't seem to understand
Why they're not strong like us.
We have Holy Ghost but it seems
We've forgotten where we came from.

Have we forgotten where we once were?
Our souls were chained to sin.
We were Satan's little helpers until
Jesus Christ stepped in.

And even after Jesus washed
Every sin we committed away.
There were times we still found it hard
To live saved from day to day.

Some nights we couldn't fall asleep
Until we had fallen on our knees,
In prayer, in tears, in weakness
Asking the Lord to hear our pleas.

And little by little with God's help
We made it to this day.
Strong in the Lord, sure of His will
We finally found our way.

We made it through by the grace of God
And through "trial and error" some days.
We also made it through with others
That helped us along the way.

So let's not forget where we came from
Until we were rescued by Jesus.
And show compassion to those still struggling
For such were some of us.

"Do you not know that the unrighteous will not inherit the kingdom of God?
Do not be deceived. Neither fornicators, nor idolaters, nor adulterers,
nor homosexuals, nor sodomites, nor thieves, nor covetous, nor drunkards,
nor revilers, nor extortioners will inherit the kingdom of God.
And such were some of you.
But you were washed, but you were sanctified, but you were justified
in the name of the Lord Jesus and by the Spirit of our God."

1 Corinthians 6:9-11

THE BREAD AND THE WINE

1 Corinthians 11:27-34

As we kneel to wash each other's feet,
As we break bread, and as we drink,
We proclaim the death of Jesus Christ.
It's much more serious than we think.

The wine represents the blood of Jesus,
And the bread, His broken body.
So before we partake we should make sure
If indeed we are worthy.

Paul says we should examine ourselves,
And judge most honestly.
If not we will condemn ourselves.
That's why so many are sick and weak.

But if we confess our sins unto God,
Repent, and be revived.
If we judge ourselves we won't be judged,
And God won't have to chastise.

We must ask Him to cleanse us deeply,
And to forgive any trespasses we have.
We must ask Him to help us straighten out,
Any relationships that have gone bad.

Make sure that all is rectified,
Before we participate,
In drinking from that blessed cup,
Or eating that blessed plate.

Therefore whoever eats this bread or drinks this cup of the Lord in an unworthy manner will be guilty of the body and blood of the Lord. But let a man examine himself, and so let him eat of the bread and drink of the cup. For he who eats and drinks in an unworthy manner eats and drinks judgment to himself, not discerning the Lord's body. For this reason many are weak and sick among you, and many sleep. For if we would judge ourselves, we would not be judged. But when we are judged, we are chastened by the Lord, that we may not be condemned with the world. Therefore, my brethren, when you come together to eat, wait for one another. But if anyone is hungry, let him eat at home, lest you come together for judgment.

1 Corinthians 11:27-34

2 Corinthians

THE CHEERFUL GIVER

2 Corinthians 9:6-7

God said if are stingy in our giving
That is how we will receive.
But if we are liberal in our giving
We will reap abundantly.

God doesn't want us to give grudgingly
Reluctantly or out of necessity
He doesn't want us to sow so sparingly
That there will be nothing for us to receive.

He loves a cheerful giver
Sow bountifully and you'll see,
That in all things and at all times
God will give you all the grace you need.

"The point is this: whoever sows sparingly will also reap sparingly, and whoever sows bountifully will also reap bountifully. Each one must give as he has decided in his heart, not reluctantly or under compulsion, for God loves a cheerful giver."
2 Corinthians 9:6-7

THE BATTLEFIELD
2 Corinthians 10:4-5

Our mind is the real battlefield,
It's our thoughts that are under attack.
Depression, distraction, and old memories
To get our focus off track.

Our enemy is Satan alone
And the demons under his control.
But our weapons are mighty through God's power
To pull down every stronghold.

We have power over our imagination
We have the power to cast down anything
That goes against what we know about God
Or that makes us sin habitually.

We serve the Lord with our minds,
Every feeling, word, and deed starts there.
Which is why we need the power of God
So we are never caught unaware.

"For the weapons of our warfare are not carnal but mighty in God for pulling down strongholds, casting down arguments and every high thing that exalts itself against the knowledge of God, bringing every thought into captivity to the obedience of Christ."

2 Corinthians 10:4-5

HIS GRACE IS SUFFICIENT

2 Corinthians 12:7-10

Paul was a great apostle,
We know that this is true.
We can learn so much from all the tests
And trials that he went through.

For the gospel of Christ, Paul endured
Danger at every hand -
From his own countrymen and from strangers
At sea and on dry land.

Paul went hungry and he went thirsty,
He also went without sufficient clothes.
He was beaten, imprisoned, and shipwrecked.
Once, he was even stoned.

Paul even had a personal tormentor
Described as a *"thorn in his flesh"*,
A messenger sent by Satan
That was with him wherever he went.

The Lord could have removed that thorn
He could have sent that demon away,
But He told Paul back in Damascus
"You will suffer for My name's sake."

So although Paul prayed three times to God
"Please remove this thorn from me,"
In a still, calm voice the Lord answered,
"My grace is sufficient for thee.

"My grace is enough for you."
Was the answer to Apostle Paul's plea.
Jesus said, *"My strength is made perfect*
Those times when you are weak."

Then Paul replied, *"Most gladly, Lord,*
I'll take pleasure in my infirmities,
So that Your power and strength
Can manifest itself through me."

What Jesus said to Apostle Paul
Applies to you and me.
God's grace is also enough for us,
It's really all that we need.

If we ever find ourselves
With a thorn in our own side,
Facing dangers and temptations
From which we cannot hide.

If it feels like others are rejoicing
While we're always going through
Tests and trials and troubles
No matter what we try to do.

Remember that we have been chosen,
To suffer for the sake of Jesus,
To be a witness to all others,
That His grace is always enough.

"And lest I should be exalted above measure by the abundance of the revelations, a thorn in the flesh was given to me, a messenger of Satan to buffet me, lest I be exalted above measure. Concerning this thing I pleaded with the Lord three times that it might depart from me. And He said to me, 'My grace is sufficient for you, for My strength is made perfect in weakness.' Therefore most gladly I will rather boast in my infirmities, that the power of Christ may rest upon me. Therefore I take pleasure in infirmities, in reproaches, in needs, in persecutions, in distresses, for Christ's sake. For when I am weak, then I am strong."

2 Corinthians 12:7-10

GALATIANS

THE FRUIT OF THE SPIRIT

Galatians 5:22-23

If you are truly a Christian
Then the Spirit of Christ dwells within
And the proof will be in your behavior
Starting with how you handle sin.

You'll love others as Christ loves you,
But of course you'll love God more.
The joy of the Lord will be your strength
If you were weak before.

Your mind will be at peace,
Because its focus will be on Christ.
You'll be patient with yourself and others
And patient as God directs your life.

Gentless and meekness will flow from you,
You'll have good things to say and do.
You'll walk by faith and not by sight,
And you'll have faith that God's word is true.

Finally, you will always be in control
Of your thoughts, your words, your deeds.
These nine attributes are the only
Proof of Christianity.

But the fruit of the Spirit is love, joy, peace, longsuffering, kindness, goodness, faithfulness, gentleness, self-control. Against such there is no law.

Galatians 5:22

MASTER OF ME

Galatians 5:24-25

My flesh wants to enjoy
Pleasures here on earth.
Never mind bending my knees in prayer
Or praise and all it's worth.

My flesh wants to indulge
In feasts of food and fun.
Forgetting the strength of fasting
Until the setting of the sun.

My flesh would rather watch a movie
Than to read God's holy word.
And Bible class instead of television
To my flesh that's just absurd.

My flesh says call my best friend
Instead of calling on the Lord in prayer.
My flesh tells me to stay home
Because I can pray anywhere.

But thank God my flesh isn't in control
Of all I say and do.
Thank God for His Holy spirit
Deep within me tried, but true.

Thank God that when I feel myself resist
Something spiritual that must be done,
I simply call on the name with all power,
The name of Jesus Christ God's son.

I call on Him to give me the strength
To walk in the spirit and not in my flesh.
I ask Him to help me not give in to temptation,
And to pass every spiritual test.

And each time He sends His anointing
Which gives me the power and strength that I need.
And He brings His word to my remembrance
To remember that my flesh isn't the master of me.

And those who are Christ's have crucified the flesh with its passions and desires.
If we live in the Spirit, let us also walk in the Spirit.
Galatians 5:24-25

EPHESIANS

SAVED BY GRACE

Ephesians 2:8-10

When I received the Holy Ghost
I knew I was saved from sin.
I had the power to live right because
I had God's power within.

I was saved from Satan because
He was no longer in control,
My life belonged to Jesus Christ
It was His blood that made me whole.

I was saved from eternal damnation
Never more to roam.
No more did I fear death because
Heaven was now my home

I thought I'd be saved from suffering
But it wasn't long before I knew,
That as Christ suffered in the flesh
There were times that I would too.

Last but not least, I realized
That I was also saved from myself.
But only if I daily died to sin
And mortified my flesh.

Then I began to grow in grace
And in the knowledge of God and His word
That's when I discovered another revelation
That I was saved to serve.

Like Christ showed us by example
Of always seeking the Father's will,
God saved me to serve Him
By assigning good works for me to fulfill.

For by grace you have been saved through faith, and that not of yourselves;
it is the gift of God, not of works, lest anyone should boast.
For we are His workmanship, created in Christ Jesus for good works,
which God prepared beforehand that we should walk in them.
Ephesians 2:8-10

THE MAN IN THE MIDDLE

Ephesians 2:14-22

Once upon a time we were dead
In trespasses and sins.
We walked according to the prince of this world
We were disobedient children.

In times past we fulfilled the desires
Of our flesh and of our mind.
By nature we were children of wrath
But that was once upon a time.

Because God who is rich in mercy
Showed unto us His great love,
By quickening us together in Christ
By lifting us up above.

God raised us together in Christ,
And made us sit in places heavenly,
So that the riches of His grace
In ages to come, all men might see.

It is by the grace of God alone,
That we have been saved through faith.
It is the gift of God given unto us
Not of our works, no matter how great.

As saved people we have been
Created in Christ to do good works,
That were ordained by God
Before the foundation of this earth.

In times past we were outsiders
Unrelated to our Lord Jesus Christ.
We were strangers to His covenant
We had no hope in our lives.

Though we were once without God in this world,
Though once we were a far off,
We have been brought together
By the blood Jesus shed on the cross.

We are no longer strangers or foreigners,
We are fellow citizens,
With direct access to the Father,
As His spiritually adopted children.

With Jesus as the chief cornerstone,
And us fitly framed together on one accord,
Built upon a holy foundation,
Of the apostles and prophets of the Lord.

"For He Himself is our peace, who has made both one, and has broken down the middle wall of separation, having abolished in His flesh the enmity, that is, the law of commandments contained in ordinances, so as to create in Himself one new man from the two, thus making peace, and that He might reconcile them both to God in one body through the cross, thereby putting to death the enmity. Now, therefore, you are no longer strangers and foreigners, but fellow citizens with the saints and members of the household of God, having been built on the foundation of the apostles and prophets, Jesus Christ Himself being the chief cornerstone, in whom the whole building, being fitted together, grows into a holy temple in the Lord, in whom you also are being built together for a dwelling place of God in the Spirit."

Ephesians 2:14-22

SEE THE SOUL

Ephesians 4:29-32

I love the young people that I lead,
And I know they know I do.
But sometimes they can't see it,
By the things I say and do.

I'd pray, *"Lord, please open their eyes,"*
Their hearts, their minds, and souls."
But, how could I worry about the mote in their eyes
Without considering the beam in my own?

A visiting preacher said, *"Your young people are bleeding,"*
But I sat in disbelief.
Until one day during noon day prayer,
The Lord Himself spoke to me.

I was praying, *"Lord, help me show your love,"*
Because I knew my approach was wrong.
When the Lord answered back to me
In a still, calm, voice that was strong:

"See the soul," He said to me.
"With your spiritual eyes, look at them.
Instead of their outer appearance,
See their souls deep down within.

"Instead of the places you know they go
And the unsaved friends they have,
Look at their empty hearts searching for Me.
Look at the sad eyes behind their laughs."

Then suddenly I saw all sorts of souls,
Dark, troubled, and all alone.
Bleeding, just like the preacher said,
Desperately in need of God's love.

Wanting to open up to us older saints,
But only being misunderstood.
Bound by pressures we've long forgotten,
As if we didn't have a childhood.

They know the doctrine, so let's move on
And parents, we can't do this alone.
What we teach in the house of God
Has got to be enforced in the home.

We must look beyond the natural
And see them with our spiritual eye.
We mustn't dwell on how they look
We must see their souls inside.

I could go on, you know I could
But I think the message is clear.
We must reach our young people with God's love,
Because the end of time is near.

"Let no corrupt word proceed out of your mouth, but what is good for necessary edification, that it may impart grace to the hearers. And do not grieve the Holy Spirit of God, by whom you were sealed for the day of redemption. Let all bitterness, wrath, anger, clamor, and evil speaking be put away from you, with all malice. And be kind to one another, tenderhearted, forgiving one another, even as God in Christ forgave you."

Ephesians 4:29-32

WE ARE AT WAR

Ephesians 6:10-18

Believe it or not we are at war
And we must not give up the fight.
For we are in spiritual battles
And we must realize:

That our fight is not with each other
I know we've heard this before.
Our only fight is with Satan
And with his demons galore.

In this fight some will lose,
And get knocked out of God's will.
Some will be left unconscious,
Some will be spiritually killed.

But God has prepared us for battle
If in His armor we dress.
So that in these last and evil days
We all can stand the test.

God has given to each of us
All the protection that we need,
From the very top of our heads
To the soles of our feet.

God's salvation is our helmet
Placed divinely upon our head,
And laid upon our chest
Is His righteousness.

God's truth is securely wrapped
Round about our waist,
And for those wicked fiery darts
Is God's shield of faith.

God has placed in our hands,
Our hearts, our minds, and souls,
The sword of the Spirit –
The mighty word of the Lord.

God wants us to stand
Strong and sure upon our feet
Walking on a solid foundation –
His precious gospel of peace.

We should continually pray for all saints
And open our mouths boldly,
To testify to everyone,
Of the gospel's mysteries.

Believe it or not, we are ready
To fight against darkness today
We can win the war in the Spirit
If God's word we fully obey.

"For we wrestle not against flesh and blood, but against principalities, against powers, against the rulers of the darkness of this world, against spiritual wickedness in high places. Wherefore take unto you the whole armor of God, that ye may be able to withstand in the evil day, and having done all, to stand. Stand therefore, having your loins girt about with truth, and having on the breastplate of righteousness; And your feet shod with the preparation of the gospel of peace; Above all, taking the shield of faith, wherewith ye shall be able to quench all the fiery darts of the wicked. And take the helmet of salvation and the sword of the Spirit, which is the word of God: Praying always with all prayer and supplication in the Spirit, And watching thereunto with all perseverance and supplication for all saints."

Ephesians 6:10-18

PHILIPPIANS

FIRST YOU PRAY

Philippians 4:6-7

We worry and we wonder
When storms blow into our life.
We moan and groan in search of
Someone in whom we can confide.

We immediately call our best friend
To tell them what we're going through.
We get angry at the world
Because we're totally confused.

We hunt down our pastor
And put our special prayer request in.
Then we sit back and wait impatiently
For our trial to come to an end.

Now, don't misunderstand me -
Most of theses things aren't wrong.
But what I want to point out is
On our knees is where we belong.

For when we first seek God out in prayer
There's a special comfort we will find.
When we kneel with faith in God
His peace will fill our mind.

We can go to God feeling so low
But His spirit will lift us up.
We can go to God feeling empty inside
And rest assured, He fills our cup.

God wants us to converse with Him daily,
Not just when things are going wrong.
Every night as we close out our day,
And every bright morning's dawn.

If we follow this pattern of living,
Of being in constant communication with Him,
He'll give us strength to face every trial
With a prayer, a praise, and a grin.

"Be anxious for nothing, but in everything by prayer and supplication,
with thanksgiving, let your requests be made known to God;
And the peace of God, which surpasses all understanding,
will guard your hearts and minds through Christ Jesus."

Philippians 4:6-7

THINK ON THESE THINGS

Philippians 4:8

Whatever things are true,
Think about them all the time,
And you will find sweet release,
And blessed peace of mind.

Whatever things are honest,
Let your thoughts dwell on only them,
And soon your words and your deeds,
Will be sincere among all men.

Whatever things are just,
Morally right and fair,
Impartial in all situations,
No matter when or where.

Whatever things are pure,
Holy, righteous and clean,
If you fill your mind with those thoughts,
Your life will be stable and serene.

Whatever things are lovely,
Pleasant, beautiful, and good,
Fill your thoughts and actions with those things
And you won't be misunderstood.

Whatever things are about good news,
That's where our thoughts should dwell,
Set aside thoughts that make you anxious,
Focus on good news you have to tell.

God's word says if you think on these things,
For the rest of all your days,
The results are sure to be,
A life of virtue and of praise.

"Finally, brethren, whatever things are true, whatever things are noble,
whatever things are just, whatever things are pure,
whatever things are lovely, whatever things are of good report,
if there is any virtue and if there is anything praiseworthy—
think on these things."

Philippians 4:8

"ALL YOU NEED"
Philippians 4:19

I remember it like it was yesterday. My company was on strike and the little bit of savings I had helped in the beginning, but almost had passed and the bills were due. I was a single parent of two teenagers and a relatively new home owner and I just didn't know what to do. I was afraid every day and a nervous wreck every night. I can see myself now, in my bedroom, daily praying and crying my heart out to God.

One day, in the midst of my cries, the voice of the Lord broke in, and said *"All you need."* I recognized those words and the scripture reference and immediately began to cry and thank the Lord. I began repeating the Bible verse over and over and, after a few days, the clouds cleared, the strike was over and I was back to work.

Once again, I was weighed down with fear, depression and anxiety and God brought me peace and freedom through the power of His word.

"And my God shall supply all your need according to His riches in glory by Christ Jesus."

Philippians 4:19

1 THESSALONIANS

A POEM OF COMFORT

1 Thessalonians 4:13-18

Shed tears because you love me,
but I'm now asleep in Jesus Christ,
I am one step closer
to my everlasting life.

Shed tears because you miss me,
but 'though I'm absent in body,
I am present with my Savior,
from this world I've been set free.

Shed tears because I'm gone now,
to the land of "No More",
No more sickness, no more pain,
and no more death, for sure.

So, shed tears of praise, and say with me
"O, death, where is your sting? -
The battle is over, the war was won,
and I've gone to meet my King!

Shed tears of joy because you know
death didn't get the victory,
I fought a good fight, and I kept the faith,
A crown now waits for me!

Shed tears of thanksgiving unto God,
He took me from labor to reward,
This was hope, this was my prayer,
this is what I was living for.

Shed tears of love, for when the trumpet sounds
and the Lord himself descends,
The dead in Christ are gonna rise first,
so we'll see each other again.

"But I do not want you to be ignorant, brethren,
concerning those who have fallen asleep,
lest you sorrow as others who have no hope.
For if we believe that Jesus died and rose again,
even so God will bring with Him those who sleep in Jesus.
For this we say to you by the word of the Lord,
that we who are alive and remain until the coming of the Lord
will by no means precede those who are asleep.
For the Lord Himself will descend from heaven with a shout,
with the voice of an archangel, and with the trumpet of God.
And the dead in Christ will rise first.
Then we who are alive and remain shall be caught up together with them in the clouds
to meet the Lord in the air.
And thus we shall always be with the Lord.
Therefore comfort one another with these words".
1 Thessalonians 4:13-18

1 Timothy

I KNOW WHAT I AM

1 Timothy 1:15

With a grateful heart,
Though I cannot understand ,
I thank God for salvation,
For I know what I am.

With every breath I take,
As my lungs expand,
I thank God for my life,
For I know what I am.

With every step that I take,
My ability to move, to walk, to stand,
I thank God for my measure of health and strength,
For I know what I am.

I am a sinner saved by grace,
Who still falls short of God's glory.
I am an earthly vessel,
With a heavenly testimony.

Of how when I was drowning in sin
God saw fit to extend His hand,
And save me from being forever lost,
In spite of who and what I am.

"This is a faithful saying and worthy of all acceptance, that Christ Jesus came into the world to save sinners, of whom I am chief."

1 Timothy 1:15

A WOMAN OF HOLINESS
1 Timothy 2:9-10

[Dedicatd to my mother with love.]

She is the kind of woman
Whose Holy Ghost is her beauty.
She can be spotted right away
Wherever she may be.

In a room of worldly women
She stands out in the crowd.
People can tell she's saved
Before she opens her mouth.

Her words are seasoned with grace.
Her cup is filled to the brim.
Her life matches the Lord's will.
She continuously praises Him.

She's an example to all women,
Not because she looks the part,
But she is a woman of holiness because
Her holiness comes from the heart.

"In like manner also, that the women adorn themselves in modest apparel, with propriety and moderation, not with braided hair or gold or pearls or costly clothing, but, which is proper for women professing godliness, with good works."

1 Timothy 2:9-10

2 TIMOTHY

FEAR NOT

2 Timothy 1:7

I've been seeking in my spirit,
And searching through my mind,
Looking for that familiar feeling,
That I haven't been able to find.

Where is that overwhelming feeling,
That grips and holds me so?
I've always had it with me,
Where it went, I do not know.

Oh, I remember now what happened,
I gave it to the Lord!
That's why I feel lighter than,
I've ever felt before.

I had it with me for so long,
I thought it would always be here.
Then one day I prayed about
My life long battle with fear.

I asked the Lord where it came from,
His word was His reply:
"God has not given you the spirit of fear,
But power, love, and a sound mind."

When that revelation hit me,
In faith to the Lord I said:
"Then I'm giving this fear to you, Lord,
Would you please just take it away?"

Instantly it lifted!
Suddenly it vanished away!
So much so that I was completely
At a loss of what to say.

Every now and then something happens,
And I begin to feel afraid.
Then I remember I traded in my fear,
For love and power and faith.

"For God has not given us a spirit of fear, but of power and of love and of a sound mind."
2 Timothy 1:7

A BODY GOD CAN USE

2 Timothy 2:20-21

God's ways much like ours
When it comes to daily hygiene.
Before He can use a person
He makes sure they are clean.

Before He sends us out to do His will,
Before we can speak for Him,
Before we can be effective in our service,
We must be clean within.

The powerful blood of Jesus,
Will clean the inner man,
The words of our mouth, the meditations of our heart,
And those feelings we don't understand.

We've got to present ourselves unto God
Acceptable and holy,
So that when God decides to use us,
We will be spiritually clean.

Our mouths must be free from hurtful words,
About our sisters and brothers.
Our hearts must be free of grudges,
That we're still holding against one another.

Our hands must be free of doing our own will,
Our feet shouldn't wander off on their own.
We must only be free in our desire to carry out
Any orders that come from God's throne.

Then we accomplish God's will.
Then we can speak out for Him.
Then we can be fit for the Master's use,
Because we will be clean within.

*"But in a great house there are not only vessels of gold and silver,
but also of wood and clay, some for honor and some for dishonor.
Therefore if anyone cleanses himself from the latter,
he will be a vessel for honor, sanctified and useful for the Master,
prepared for every good work."*

2 Timothy 2:20-21

HEBREWS

BY FAITH

Hebrews 11:1

A few months ago in Bible class,
Our pastor was teaching on faith,
From the 11th chapter of Hebrews,
Which reads like the Hall of Fame.

I almost tuned completely out,
Because I knew the chapter by heart.
"By faith Abraham led by God,
Went on a journey to make a new start."

So there I was ignoring bible class,
When the Lord spoke right to me:
"What have you done by faith?"
He asked me quietly.

While the pastor went on teaching,
I was stinging from the Lord's rebuke.
Inwardly repenting for my lack of respect,
For sitting in His house with that attitude.

While the Bible class continued,
I took out a notebook and pen,
And wrote the words *"By faith Patricia..."*
Over and over again.

I sat there wondering to myself,
What have I done by faith?
In that moment I could only come up with
The fact that by faith I was saved.

As the class went on, I picked the pen back up,
And thought about what faith meant to me.
Then after awhile, I wrote these words:
"By faith Patricia published a book of poetry."

I stared at those eight little words
Until they began to sink in.
I'm not sure how longer it was
Before the Bible class came to an end.

As I packed up to go home,
I didn't realize what had happened to me.
But from that one on one Bible class with God,
I had been implanted with a divine seed.

And from that seed my faith grew,
Along with God's favor and mercy,
Just like I wrote in my notebook,
I published my first book of poetry.

"Now faith is the substance of things hoped for, the evidence of things not seen."
Hebrews 11:1

"WHAT HAVE YOU DONE BY FAITH?"

Hebrews 11:6

One night I was sitting in Bible class waiting for things to get started, like I had a hundred of times before. Eventually we were told to *"turn to the 11th chapter of Hebrews and let's begin reading together."* I turned to the chapter as directed, but promptly tuned out thinking, *"Oh, he's teaching on faith again."* I reached into my tote bag, pulled out my notebook and began turning the pages, reviewing my many to do lists.

I wasn't reading along (or even listening) but I could hear the congregation reading in the background. After a few moments, subconsciously I began to listen, and all I could hear them saying was *"by faith"* this and *"by faith"* that. I sighed and went back to my notebook. Then the Lord's rebuke broke through my disobedient spirit and said, *"What have **you** done by faith?"* I turned to a blank page in my notebook and I wrote 'By faith Patricia' and stopped. Tears filled my eyes and fear filled my heart. How dare I disobey the instruction to read God's word? How dare I blow off a Bible lesson thinking I'd heard it all before? How dare I sit in God's house with such a haughty spirit? Obviously, God was not pleased with me.

The 11th chapter of Hebrews is like a recap of the great heroes of the Old Testament—all they obeyed, all they accomplished, and all they endured, all by faith. God's question came back to me again: *"What have you done by faith?"* Again I wrote *"By faith Patricia"* but this time continued writing the words 'published her first book of poetry' and stopped writing. Right then and there the faith to publish my first book, A Time To Write, was born. That was September of 2008. A Time to Write was released in March of 2010. Isn't it just like God to turn a chastisement into a blessing?

"But without faith it is impossible to please Him, for he who comes to God must believe that He is, and that He is a rewarder of those who diligently seek Him."

Hebrews 11:6

THE HALL OF FAITH

Hebrews 11:2; 12:1

By faith Abel's sacrifice
Was more excellent that Cain's.
God gave Abel respect
And for that he was slain.

By faith Enoch pleased God,
So when it was time for his eternal rest,
God translated him and took him up,
Through his faith he did not see death.

Noah built that famous ark,
He too had enormous faith.
God warned him that destruction was coming
But in Noah He found grace.

Faith took Abraham to a strange land,
And by faith he would have sacrificed his son.
The one that he and his wife longed for
But in the end, by faith, they won.

Moses chose to suffer affliction
Rather than the pleasures of sin for a season.
He led the Israelites through the wilderness
His faith in God was the reason.

And how about that wall of Jericho
Falling down after seven days?
The men of war, the holy priests,
And Joshua all walked around by faith.

And like the one who wrote Hebrews,
I just don't have enough time to tell,
Of the faith of Rahab, Gideon, Daniel,
King David and Samuel.

All of those Old Testament heroes,
All of the miracles God performed
Seas were divided, boys fought giants
Bushes and furnances that could not burn.

This world wasn't even worthy of them,
They made mountains and caves their homes.
Some of them were tortured,
Others were imprisoned and stoned,

Now with so many witnesses before us,
We can lay aside every weight,
And every sin that tempts us,
And endeavor to walk by faith.

"For by it [faith] the elders obtained a good testimony.
And these all, having obtained a good report through faith,
received not the promise: God having provided some better thing for us,
that they without us should not be made perfect.
Therefore we also, since we are surrounded by so great a cloud of witnesses,
let us lay aside every weight, and the sin which so easily ensnares us."

Hebrews 11:2; 12:1

LAY IT ASIDE

Hebrews 12:1

Dear Lord, I am so heavy
Burdened with a load of care.
The weight of the world on my shoulder
Is too much for me to bear.

Dear Lord, I am so heavy,
It's too hard to get from here to there.
Every step I take is too painful,
It's even hard to kneel in prayer.

I've been waiting for You to move
All of these burdens and cares.
Feels like my prayers just go to the ceiling,
Seems like my voice You don't hear.

What was that Lord,
You want me to read
Hebrews 12:1 to find the answer
To the strength I say I need?

Selah.

Lord, I understand now ,
What it is You're trying to say.
It's up to me to do the lifting,
It's up to me to lay aside the weight.

And look to you for mercy,
Favor, love, and grace
For you alone are the author
And finisher of my faith.

*"Therefore we also, since we are surrounded by so great a cloud of witnesses,
let us lay aside every weight, and the sin which so easily ensnares us,
and let us run with endurance the race that is set before us."*

Hebrews 12:1

BEYOND THE CROSS

Hebrews 12:2

From the moment the world began,
To the sinful fall of man,
He looked beyond the cross.

From the last prophet to stand,
To the nails in His hand,
He looked beyond the cross.

From His birth being old scriptures fulfilled,
To His meat simply being to do His Father's will,
He looked beyond the cross.

From the betrayer's silver-coined fee,
To the garden of Gethsemane,
He looked beyond the cross.

From being beaten and abused,
To being falsely accused,
He looked beyond the cross.

He ascended to make intercession for me,
Seeing my place in eternity,
He looked beyond the cross.

Enduring the pain and the shame,
He looked beyond the cross.
For the joy set before Him
He paid the ultimate cost.

Beyond my faults too many to mention,
Beyond the cross to my redemption.
Beyond all of my sinful temptations,
Beyond the cross to my salvation.

So I will look beyond my cross,
Beyond all I don't understand.
I will look beyond my cross,
Straight to His nail scarred hands.

I will look beyond my cross,
To my joys and good days.
I will look beyond my cross,
Beyond my sickness and pain.

I will look beyond my cross,
Beyond my doubts and fears,
To how He's blessed me,
Down through the years.

I will look beyond my cross,
To my victory.
I will look beyond my cross,
To all He's done for me.

"Looking unto Jesus, the author and finisher of our faith, who for the joy that was set before Him endured the cross, despising the shame, and has sat down at the right hand of the throne of God."

Hebrews 12:2

JAMES

COUNT IT ALL JOY

James 1:2; 12-15 | 1 John 2:1

God's word says that he who endures
Temptations when he is tried
The Lord himself has promised
That he will receive the crown of life.

Temptation is the trying of my faith,
Designed to produce patience deep within,
So that I may be mature and complete,
And not lacking anything.

Some wonder if God is tempting them,
But God's word says this isn't so
God may test, but He does not tempt.
Here's how it really goes:

We actually tempt ourselves,
We are enticed by our own lusts,
And when our lust comes to fruition it causes us to sin
And the result of that is a spiritual death.

Satan may plant a thought in our mind,
But he has no power to make it stay there.
We have the power to rebuke the thought,
We don't have to fall for the dare.

We already know we will be tempted
But we can count it all joy as we go through
God left us a complete road map
His word is a way out for me and for you.

"My brethren, count it all joy when you fall into various trials,
knowing that the testing of your faith produces patience."

James 1:2-3

"Blessed is the man who endures temptation; for when he has been approved, he will receive the crown of life which the Lord has promised to those who love Him. Let no one say when he is tempted, "I am tempted by God"; for God cannot be tempted by evil, nor does He Himself tempt anyone. But each one is tempted when he is drawn away by his own desires and enticed. Then, when desire has conceived, it gives birth to sin; and sin, when it is full-grown, brings forth death."

James 1:12-15

"My little children, these things I write to you, so that you may not sin. And if anyone sins, we have an Advocate with the Father, Jesus Christ the righteous."

1 John 2:1

GOD WANTS MORE

James 1:22-25

We sing praises to God
Of how He brought us through.
They sound almost as sweet
As the morning dew.

We read God's word everyday
And commit it to memory.
We quote our favorite passages
We even know what they mean.

God wants more than memorized verses,
He wants to find His word deep in our heart.
He wants our actions to always line up with
The words that we daily impart.

But God wants more than praises,
He wants our lives to sing of Him.
He wants us to be living witnesses
Of how to live free from the power of sin.

"But be doers of the word, and not hearers only, deceiving yourselves. For if anyone is a hearer of the word and not a doer, he's like a man observing his natural face in a mirror; for he observes himself, goes away, and immediately forgets what kind of man he was. But he who looks into the perfect law of liberty and continues in it, and is not a forgetful hearer but a doer of the work, this one will be blessed in what he does."
James 1:22-25

LET GOD BE GOD

James 4:13-16

We all want to express our opinions.
We want everyone to hear and see,
What we think about this or that ,
How we think things should be.

We sit and think about our future,
And of how things are coming along.
Then in midstream we change our plans,
Because the road we're on seems wrong.

We get upset when tests and trials come.
We try to figure out why,
We analyze, we rationalize, we criticize,
We sulk, we moan, we cry.

We aim and take our own best shot,
When the powers of darkness strike.
Then when we get knocked out,
We feel ready to give up the fight.

God can meet each and every need,
Inside each and every one of us.
But He will only meet those needs,
If we surrender all to Jesus.

He who keeps his tongue, keeps his life
That proverb took care of our opinions.
And planning our futures is something over which
God should always have complete dominion.

You don't have to fight your own battles,
Rest assured in the certainty of God's love.
Be filled with God's sweet Holy Spirit,
And rely on the power of the blood.

When the powers of darkness
Have the nerve to step in front of you,
Remember that nothing in this world ,
Is greater than He who's inside of you.

"Come now, you who say, 'Today or tomorrow we will go to such and such a city, spend a year there, buy and sell, and make a profit';whereas you do not know what will happen tomorrow. For what is your life? It is even a vapor that appears for a little time and then vanishes away. Instead you ought to say, "If the Lord wills, we shall live and do this or that." But now you boast in your arrogance. All such boasting is evil."

James 4:13-16

DOUBLE MINDED

James 4:3,8

"You ask Me to daily bless you,
So I give you twenty-four hours in a day,
But all you can spare for Me is fifteen minutes,
To fall on your knees and pray.

"You ask Me to open your understanding,
So I bless you with a pastor well read.
I increase his knowledge of Me word,
And you have the nerve to say you're not being fed.

"You ask Me to bless your entire church,
So I give you an abundance of gifts to use.
But you only come on Sundays,
Or when there's something of interest to you.

"You ask Me to help you spread My word,
But when I send sinners your way,
You raise your eyebrows and stick up your nose,
As if they're someone that can't be saved.

"However My word says to give cheerfully,
But tithes and offerings you rarely bring,
You never cease to ask me to bless you,
With the best of everything.

"When you need protection and deliverance,
As always, I'm right there,
But through it all you have the nerve to say
I have yet to answer your prayers."

"You ask and do not receive, because you ask amiss, that you may spend it on your pleasures. Cleanse your hands, you sinners; and purify your hearts, you double-minded."

James 4:3,8

1 Peter

CHOSEN VESSELS

1 Peter 2:9-10

Once there was a wise old collector,
And His specialty was in antiques,
He would look high and He would look low,
For things He thought were unique.

Many of the places he visited,
Folks didn't understand why,
He was always picking up items,
That didn't quite catch their eye.

He'd pick up a rusty utensil,
He'd snatch up a faded old dish,
He'd go out of His way to purchase,
Vessels full of cracks, stains and chips.

You see this man was a wise collector,
He could see past the rust and the dirt,
When He looked at an item He imagined,
How it would look once He got to work.

He restored antique pieces,
He polished vintage tin,
Smiling all along because He knew,
Just the spot He would put it in.

One day He found an empty vessel
And later it turned out to be
Not a dish, or a jar, or a bottle
It turned out to be you and me.

We are God's chosen vessels,
We've been made fit for the Master's use,
There's a job specifically designed by God,
For each and every one of us to do.

"But you are a chosen generation, a royal priesthood, a holy nation, His own special people, that you may proclaim the praises of Him who called you out of darkness into His marvelous light; who once were not a people but are now the people of God, who had not obtained mercy but now have obtained mercy."

1 Peter 2:9-10

2 Peter

THE THREE R's OF SALVATION

2 Peter 1:5-11

A good education is founded on
Three simple but important rules:
Reading, [w]riting and [a]rithmetic
Commonly called the Three R's of school.

No matter how great you sing in the glee club,
Or how well you can debate,
Even if you're the class president,
If you can't read and write you won't graduate.

No matter how many touchdowns,
Or how many trophies you have running track.
If you can't add, subtract, multiply and divide
You'll just keep getting left back.

The same can be said for salvation.
It might interest you to know,
That there are also Three R's in Christ,
And this is how it goes:

First, *Receive the Holy ghost,*
Without it you are lost.
Jesus wants to dwell within you
For your sins He paid the cost.

Second, *Reach out to God in prayer.*
Keep in constant communication with Christ
He will lead, guide and direct
Every area of your life.

Third, *Read God's word.*
Hide it in the corners of your heart.
Not only the famous and familiar verses
But every single part.

These are the Three R's of Salvation
And if you're missing any of them today,
Just like the Three R's of education
You will not graduate.

No matter the choirs you sing with,
Or the auxiliary groups you're in,
If you don't follow these three rules
You will not make it to heaven.

"But also for this very reason, giving all diligence, add to your faith virtue, to virtue knowledge, to knowledge self-control, to self-control perseverance, to perseverance godliness, to godliness brotherly kindness, and to brotherly kindness love. For if these things are yours and abound, you will be neither barren nor unfruitful in the knowledge of our Lord Jesus Christ. For he who lacks these things is shortsighted, even to blindness, and has forgotten that he was cleansed from his old sins. Therefore, brethren, be even more diligent to make your call and election sure, for if you do these things you will never stumble; for so an entrance will be supplied to you abundantly into the everlasting kingdom of our Lord and Savior Jesus Christ."

2 Peter 1:5-11

1 John

THE POWER OF THE BLOOD

1 John 1:7,9

There's power in the blood of Jesus
To wash your sins away.
To cleanse sinful thoughts from your mind
And to sanctify the words you say.

Power from the moment of salvation
When the Lord God takes control,
And with the tongue you praise Him
In a language that's unknown.

You're filled with power that prepares you
For whatever is to come.
Power from the rising
To the setting of the sun.

Power that gives you a fresh anointing
To do God's divine will.
Power to pray in the spirit
Power in His salvation to stand still.

Power that comes from the blood
Jesus shed on Calvary that day.
Power to protect you
No harm can come your way.

Power to forgive you
When you stumble now and then.
Power to restore your soul
If you find yourself back in sin.

Power that Satan will run from
But power by which you can stand
In the face of any temptation
Knowing that Satan can't lay a hand.

Power that makes it possible
For all sinners to be free.
The wages of sin is eternal death
But Jesus paid the penalty.

There's power in the blood of Jesus
When the Holy Ghost come in.
Power in the blood of Jesus
That this world can't comprehend.

"But if we walk in the light as He is in the light, we have fellowship with one another, and the blood of Jesus Christ His Son cleanses us from all sin.
If we confess our sins, He is faithful and just to forgive us our sins and to cleanse us from all unrighteousness."

1 John 1:7

REVELATION

HOMEGOING

Revelation 14:12-13

The death of someone that you know
Can be quite a sad affair;
Whether it's sudden or prolonged
It still brings feelings of despair.

Most people see the loss of a loved one
As the end of that person's road.
In sorrow they remember
And in grief they carry the load.

"You've only got one life to live," they say.
"So do your living well."
"You only go around once," they say.
Dismissing heaven and hell.

But how you live your life on earth,
What you say and what you do,
Will determine where you spend eternity,
And will determine just with who.

If you let Jesus live within you now,
You'll live forevermore with Him.
But your soul will forever burn forever if
You live your life in sin.

For those of us who die in Christ,
It's as if we're going home,
To dwell in paradise forever,
To view God upon His throne.

Where will you live when you die?
Who will you live with eternally?
It's best to live for Christ right now.
Otherwise, well, you'll see.

"Here is the patience of the saints;
here are those who keep the commandments of God and the faith of Jesus.
Then I heard a voice from heaven saying to me, "
Write: 'Blessed are the dead who die in the Lord from now on.'
'Yes,' says the Spirit, 'that they may rest from their labors, and their works follow them.'"
Revelation 14:12-13

NEW JERUSALEM
Revelation 21:1-4

There will be a new heaven and a new earth-
A brand Nnew Jerusalem
Coming out of heaven dressed like a bride
Prepared for her husband.

There will be no more crying, no more tears,
No more death, sorrow, or pain.
He that overcometh on earth
Will never be hungry or thirsty again.

There will be a tree of life that will bear fruit,
With leaves that will heal every nation.
We shall freely drink of the water
That flows from an everlasting fountain.

There will be no need for candles or lamps,
For the glory of God shall be our light.
This city will have no sun, moon or stars,
And time won't be separated by night.

The nations of those who are saved by God,
Will forever reign with Him,
In that city where the Lamb dwells in the temple,
In the New Jerusalem.

"Now I saw a new heaven and a new earth, for the first heaven and the first earth had passed away. Also there was no more sea. Then I, John, saw the holy city, New Jerusalem, coming down out of heaven from God, prepared as a bride adorned for her husband. And I heard a loud voice from heaven saying, 'Behold, the tabernacle of God is with men, and He will dwell with them, and they shall be His people. God Himself will be with them and be their God. And God will wipe away every tear from their eyes; there shall be no more death, nor sorrow, nor crying. There shall be no more pain, for the former things have passed away.'"

Revelation 21:1-4

About the Author

"After working for more than 20 years in the telecommunications industry and becoming an expert on customer service, I realized I wanted **more**. My first move was to a non-profit agency where my organizational skills could shine. Five years later funding problems developed, resulting in a lay-off I didn't see coming.

"My next move was to a small radio station. While there, I worked part-time for a few months at a local library and a women's shelter. I also began teaching writing classes at a senior living facility. Almost a decade later, I had mastered just about every facet of broadcasting, but I still wanted **more**. So, I accepted a full-time sales job at a larger radio station and a short time later - a part-time mentoring position with an agency for inner city at-risk teens.

After a chain of life-altering events - including a near death experience - through divine intervention I realized it was time for me to pursue my passion for writing. After all, that passion was why five years earlier I had become an author. It's why writing copy was one of my favorite responsibilities at the radio station. It's why my fondest memories of the time I spent with the at-risk teens were the journal and poetry sessions. And it's why no matter what was going on in my life, I had never stopped teaching those writing classes at the senior living facility.

"Today I am living out my passion for writing and publishing. In addition to authoring eight titles of my own,

I find joy in pouring over the manuscripts - mostly handwritten - of seniors who want to publish their memoirs. The thrill of helping them rekindle long forgotten memories, the pleasure of reading their stories, and the satisfaction of seeing those stories in print, is the **more** that I've been longing for."

PATRICIA MIDDLETON
"I've written my vision; let me help you write yours."

BOOKS BY PATRICIA MIDDLETON

A TIME TO WRITE (2010)
Inspirational Poems and Songs of Worship.

WORDS WILL NEVER HURT ME (2013)
A Memoir About Overcoming Childhood Memories of Domestic Violence

THE WRITING WAS ON THE WALL (2013)
A Memoir About the Early Warning Signs of Dating Violence

POETIC PRAISE (2016)
For Seasons of Singleness

LOVE LINES (2016)
Inspirational Wedding Poems

WORDBEATS (2016)
Pulsations of a Young Poet's Heart

MR. WRITE (2019)
Poems of Love and Loss

FIFTY MINUTES OF GRACE (2020)
Testimonies of God's Undeserved Favor

WRITE THE VISION PUBLISH THE DREAM (2022)
Introduction to Self Publishing

BURIED WORDS (2022)
Finding the Faith to Tell Your Story

MORE INK FOR THE PEN (2022)
New and Selected Poems

PROLOGUE

The title of this book comes from the account in Matthew 4:1-10 (and Luke 4:1-12) of the temptation of Jesus in the wilderness.

> *Then Jesus was led up by the Spirit into the wilderness to be tempted by the devil. And when He had fasted forty days and forty nights, afterward He was hungry. Now when the tempter came to Him, he said "If You are the Son of God, command that these stones become bread." But He answered and said, "**It is written**, 'Man shall not live by bread alone, but by every word that proceeds from the mouth of God.'" [Deuteronomy 8:3]*
>
> *Then the devil took Him up into the holy city, set Him on the pinnacle of the temple, and said to Him, "If You are the Son of God, throw Yourself down. For it is written: 'He shall give His angels charge over you,' and, 'In their hands they shall bear you up, Lest you dash your foot against a stone.'" Jesus said to him, "**It is written**, 'You shall not tempt the LORD your God.'" [Deuteronomy 6:16]*
>
> *Again, the devil took Him up on an exceedingly high mountain, and showed Him all the kingdoms of the world and their glory. And he said to Him, "All these things I will give You if You will fall down and worship me." Then Jesus said to him, "Away with you Satan! **It is written**, 'You shall worship the LORD your God, and Him only you shall serve.'"*
> *[Deuteronomy 6:13]*

It's interesting to note that Jesus faced these temptations immediately following His water and Spirit baptism (Matthew 3:13-17), yet, once in the wilderness, He didn't rely on the strength of those experiences. With each temptation, Jesus relied on the word of God, specifically from the book of Deuteronomy—the same book that recaps the wilderness journey of the children of Israel.

In doing so, Jesus left us an example to follow—a principle for us to live by. When we find ourselves in a wilderness season, faced with the tests, trials, and temptations of the devil, we should always rely on God's word rather than our own spiritual strength. With each temptation, there will always be an answer in the word of God that will strengthen us and weaken our adversary.

My prayer is that the poems and testimonies in this book will not only uplift and inspire you, but also lead you directly to the word of God. For it is there that you will find the strength, the love, the peace, and the direction that you've been searching for. *It Is Written.*